My Personal
Holocaust

Triumphing Over the Devastation

of Trauma-Based Mind Control

CAROLYN SHERROW

ILLUMIFY
MEDIA.COM

My Personal Holocaust

Copyright © 2024 by Carolyn Sherrow

All rights reserved. No part of this book may be reproduced in any form or by any means—whether electronic, digital, mechanical, or otherwise—without permission in writing from the publisher, except by a reviewer, who may quote brief passages in a review.

The views and opinions expressed in this book are those of the author and do not necessarily reflect the official policy or position of Illumify Media Global.

Scripture quotations marked TPT are taken from The Passion Translation. The Passion Translation® is a registered trademark of Passion & Fire Ministries, Inc. Copyright © 2020 Passion & Fire Ministries, Inc. Scripture quotations marked NIV are taken from the Holy Bible, New International Version®, NIV® Copyright ©1973, 1978, 1984, 2011 by Biblica, Inc.® Used by permission. All rights reserved worldwide. Scripture quotations marked NKJV are taken from the New King James Version®. Copyright © 1982 by Thomas Nelson. Used by permission. All rights reserved. Scripture quotations marked ASV are taken from the American Standard Version (public domain). Scripture quotations marked NASB are taken from the New American Standard Bible®, Copyright © 1960, 1971, 1977, 1995, 2020 by The Lockman Foundation. All rights reserved. Scripture quotations marked KJV are taken from the Holy Bible, King James Version (public domain)." Scripture quotations marked LITV are taken from the literal translation of the Holy Bible, Copyright 1976-2000 by Jay P Green, Sr.

Published by
Illumify Media Global
www.IllumifyMedia.com
"Let's bring your book to life!"

Library of Congress Control Number: 2024920479

Paperback ISBN: 978-1-964251-19-6

Cover design by Debbie Lewis

Printed in the United States of America

Contents

My Personal Holocaust: Origin of the Title v
Acknowledgments vii
Foreword by Bruce John Miller ix
Introduction xv

1 Discovery 1
2 Fear 9
3 Shame 19
4 Transitions 30
5 Perceptions 40
6 The Truth Will Set You Free 50
7 False versus True Memories 59
8 The Science of Memory 68
9 Grief 80
10 Identity Theft 92
11 Alters versus Little Ones 102
12 Demons 111
13 False jesus 123
14 Why 134
15 Healing Love 146
16 Forgiveness 157
17 Reintegration 170
18 The End 181

Epilogue 183
Appendix A: A Summary for Survivors 186

Appendix B: A Summary for Counselors 194
Appendix C: A Summary for Church Leaders 200
Bibliography 205
About the Author 206
Notes 209

My Personal Holocaust:
Origin of the Title

Rick Wienecke is a talented and anointed Israeli sculptor. His pièce de resistance is an incredible creation titled *Fountain of Tears* (referencing Jeremiah 9:1); this piece and much of Wienecke's other work relates to the Holocaust. Available on YouTube is a moving video about the *Fountain of Tears* creation, narrated by the artist.

Nearly twenty years ago, I attended a prophetic conference during which Rick was one of the presenters. I visited his display room at midday and found a small sculpture that moved me so deeply I hated to put it back on the table. He came over to answer any questions I might have.

"I need to tell you what this does to me," I said, choking back the tears.

Rick encouraged me to tell him more.

After regaining my composure, I told him about my background.

Rick listened to my story without judgment and grasped the depth of my pain. Then he responded from his heart, "Oh, a personal holocaust."

And so it was.

holocaust (*n.*)

: a great or complete devastation or destruction (dictionary.com)

: a very large amount of destruction (Cambridge Dictionary)

Acknowledgments

With tremendous gratitude to Nancy Rue, mentor and friend. You have always accepted and encouraged me, both personally and as a writer, and then you helped me with this difficult project. You are a major blessing!

To all my prayer supporters: Dawn, Desi and Nina, Donna, Kim, Maryanne, Matt, Aimee, Loretta, and the Colorado Scribblies. I know I've missed some of your names, but please know I truly appreciate you all.

To my counselors: I couldn't have reached this level of healing without your teamwork, faith, and encouragement.

To the triune God: I am still learning about Your many aspects and will never stop this side of heaven. You've healed me with Your boundless yet accessible truth and love.

Foreword

I first encountered the reality of satanic ritual abuse (SRA) while working for a Christian ministry in Colorado. Trained to facilitate the one-hour small group prayer sessions in the Family Foundations International seminar, "From Curse to Blessing," I had been forewarned not to attempt to engage with survivors of SRA. The seminar's focus was to pray (briefly) for anyone whose emotional wounds had surfaced following the prior teaching of Craig Hill—wounds caused by abandonment, rejection, sexual or physical abuse, and so on. It was encouraging to witness people receiving freedom as memories of early trauma surfaced and then God healed the roots of bondage that resulted from those wounds. However, none of us prayer ministers were prepared to deal with the shock of listening to someone whose memories included torture, rape, child sacrifice, being buried alive, pedophilia, and more. We were woefully unprepared for this kind of horrific abuse and thus were instructed to refer folks who had suffered such abuse to the "professionals."

"Could this kind of evil be happening in America today?" you may ask. "Are these memories real?" I've witnessed it firsthand from more than twenty-five different survivors, and they all ask the same questions: "Am I making this up? Or am I just crazy?" The excruciating pain associated with those memories certainly is real! I always respond by telling victims, "No one makes up memories with this level of pain associated with the memory—it's real." Of course, the reason such victims think they're "going crazy" is because they've had no recollection of these terrible events for most of their young lives. Then, suddenly, memories surface, often not until survivors are thirty-five to forty-five years old.

I believe that God was preparing me to deal with this level of trauma since my high school days. At that time, because I had Jewish friends, I read about the brutal treatment of Jews in Hitler's death camps. I still remember the gruesome stories of surgeries performed—*without* anesthesia—on innocent Jewish children by Nazi doctor Josef Mengele. The result was a shattering of the mind whereby each child would become "split" -one part holding on to the traumatic memory, the other part experiencing complete amnesia. The amnesic barrier would then be reinforced again and again through repetitive trauma, allowing the child to "survive" the trauma without any recollection of it at all. Nevertheless, Dr. Mengele discovered he could "access" the traumatized part of the child's mind and control the child at will.

Sadly, Dr. Mengele—a.k.a. the angel of death—escaped to South America after World War II, and his experimental research survived to be used by equally evil humans.

It's common knowledge today that in America this kind of intentional, systematic, extreme trauma has not only been performed on children by self-proclaimed Satanists, but also by certain clandestine government agencies as well as members of religious groups and men's fraternities, such as the Freemasons. In fact, because of the diversity of methods now being used for programming their victims, the name among professional therapists for this kind of abuse was changed from SRA to TBMC (trauma-based mind control).

Foreword

Programming of young children today, however, is exponentially more sophisticated and diabolical than Mengele ever thought possible.

So, does this mean that we are to just consider these survivors as *hopeless cases*? Certainly not! Nevertheless, the sobering truth is that these precious souls require much more than an FFI seminar and a few weeks, months, or even years of therapy to be freed of the years of extensive programming. Indeed, they face a very long road to recovery. Not only do they think they are "going crazy" because of bizarre nightmares, body memories, and terrifying flashbacks, but whenever they have the courage to share these things with those in "the church," they are often treated like lepers—shunned or ignored. Often, no one in the "ministry" knows what to do. Could it be that the only solution is to simply turn such survivors over to the professional psychiatrist?

I must admit that, at first, all of us prayer ministers were at a loss as to what to do.

It wasn't long, however, until we discovered several ministries that had already been training counselors for years on how to deal with this sophisticated sort of abuse. Dr. Ed Smith, whose truth-based prayer method was so very effective in setting captives free, was becoming an authority in the field. He taught a weeklong seminar (which I was fortunate enough to attend) on the subject. However, to emphasize the seriousness, complexity, and profound weightiness of this type of prayer ministry, the very first day Ed warned the group, "If God hasn't clearly TOLD YOU to be involved in helping these survivors, then DON'T DO IT!"

Why the stern warning? Survivors have been programmed to never trust anyone representing the Lord

Jesus Christ and have been further told that Jesus Himself hates them and will abandon them because they are evil. This alone would prevent people from making any therapeutic progress whatsoever! Then, when the minister gives up and refers them to another therapist, the survivors' programming is reinforced. One lady told me after six months of weekly sessions, "So, when are you going to leave me?"

Nevertheless, survivors continue to receive healing across America and around the world because of the persistence of caring ministers and the unfailing power of the Holy Spirit.

One of these survivors is Carolyn Sherrow. She is by far one of the most courageous, fiercely focused, funny, smart, and successful Christian women I've ever known. When I worked with her at Family Foundations International, she was working as a PA at Kaiser Permanente. At the time, I had little understanding of how hard she'd worked to achieve her goals in life and how much respect she had earned due to her position as a woman in this traditionally male-dominated profession. In fact, one day she had to correct me—rather sternly, as I remember—because I was so ignorant of the nature of her professional expertise. I, in my ignorance, had introduced her to someone as a "physician's assistant" (diploma and certification) instead of referring to her by the accurate and significantly different title, "physician assistant" (master's degree). Carolyn reminds me of the incident (with a chuckle) to this day.

So, in conclusion, one must take to heart that the life of this amazing woman is absolute proof that despite years of painful abuse, self-loathing, shame, and confusion, Carolyn fought the "good fight of faith" until she ultimately found freedom and a joy-filled future (see 1 Timothy 6:12 KJV).

Foreword

This is what I hope you will discover and appreciate as you read her memoir.

Carolyn's carefully researched and well-written true story is also a testimony to the healing power of the love of Jesus Christ. I believe that it will provide hope for the hopeless and needed encouragement for those attempting to minister to many precious survivors. Furthermore, in my opinion, every pastor should read *My Personal Holocaust* and preach sermons from its contents so that their church can offer support, prayer, and a sanctuary for survivors in their congregation. In the end, thankfully, we remain confident that "God causes all things to work together for good to those who love God, to those who are called according to His purpose" (Romans 8:28 NASB).

Bruce John Miller
Lite-Heart Ministries Inc.

Introduction

When I was not quite three years old, my father came home one day and announced that the family was moving out of state—no explanation. He had already scouted ahead and found a few houses my parents would choose between, checked out school districts, and arranged a job for himself. Mom always figured all this preparation was because he wanted to move closer to where he loved to fish, but that was just a guess. And as a good wife in the 1950s, she didn't press for details. She just got her family ready for the move.

I don't know if my father realized something awful was happening to me or if God gave him a strong nudge to get me out of the geographical area. What my father didn't know was that I was a target of trauma-based mind control–otherwise known as ritual abuse. And he couldn't know that a dissociative disorder would result from what had been done to me.

What you are about to read is my history, but no longer my identity.

My purpose in writing this book was not to elicit sympathy or admiration but to give hope for healing to anyone who has suffered trauma, ritual or otherwise. So many survivors have lost hope. I know I did.

I write this book to encourage survivors to continue the fight and to look ahead to a healed future.

I write it to fulfill the command of Ephesians 5:11: "Have nothing to do with the fruitless deeds of darkness, but instead expose them" (NIV). And I like to add, "Don't ignore them and hope they go away!" I never asked for this fight, but here it is.

Finally, I write this book to call attention to God's love and healing power. Where man's efforts had failed, God triumphed. Only He could have taken an emotionally shattered yet highly functional, dissociative forty-five-year-old adolescent (for that is what I was) and healed her so completely, growing her up into the woman He created her to be: His beloved daughter, warrior, and teacher of His truth.

God directed me to the people and ministries I needed to help accomplish that transformation. As my counselor, "John" emphasized, we were a team—him, God, and me—working in tandem so that I could receive truth, love, and healing. We became a "threefold cord" in the nine-year struggle (see Ecclesiastes 4:12 KJV). This was added to the thirty months of my working with "Phoebe," who first realized I was dissociative and who started me on my journey.

This book is my personal story. It isn't a scientific dissertation or an exposé of conspiracy theories. Above all, it is not sensationalized. It is very real.

I've tried to make the book rational and clear, knowing how incredibly difficult this subject is; a great deal of misinformation is out there. I pray this book will be helpful for those who are experiencing symptoms of dissociation, diagnosed or not.

This book is, of course, nonfiction. However, some scenes have been fictionalized for readability. It's pretty hard to describe what happened inside my own head

Introduction

without adding some details. Honestly, it would've been nice to have some mental photographs available.

You will notice seven poems scattered throughout the work. I wrote these as a form of self-therapy and to express the inexpressible thoughts and feelings I had while on the long healing journey. They act rather like journal entries correlating with the chapters that follow them.

My counselor, John, had a superb habit of taking notes on his laptop during our sessions and then printing them out for me. I happily accepted them and have kept them to this day (I have six large three-ring binders full!). I've used excerpts from them as illustration in most chapters.

Allow me to clarify my use of the font changes you will see in those excerpts:

Italics usually indicate a "little one" is speaking, or I am narrating what the little one is saying or feeling. You will note the grammar is often incorrect, but that is how each of these individuals spoke.

There are times when I have had to set the scene or explain what had happened just before it; those explanations are generally noted in normal font. When additional clarity is needed, the speaker is labeled.

When I was researching the session notes, I realized the little ones spoke mostly when they or we felt strong, painful emotions, such as fear or rage, and the calmer and more logical passages generally reflect my narration.

I use the terms "little ones" and "parts" interchangeably. I prefer "little ones" because it's more descriptive of the guardians—they are, after all, children. "Parts" always brings me mentally back to body parts from my medical days. Talk about a distraction!

"Alters" refers to alternate personalities—these are more mature, more complex, and of different ages (discussed in chapter 10)

Times New Roman font generally denotes the counselor speaking. John usually asked me questions about what I was feeling, hearing, and so on, but quite often spoke directly to the little ones through me. You will find more illustration as to how he worked distributed throughout the body of the book.

This book is organized by subject matter rather than chronologically, so you may notice some jumping around. When dates are listed, they are accurate to the month of the session involved. I have no way of knowing exactly when certain traumatic events occurred. Many of them were revisited several times in different sessions. God's mercy wouldn't let me be harmed or re-traumatized.

Most names have been changed, but all events are as accurate as I can make them. Some events have been condensed or partially fictionalized within the book's timeline for the sake of clarity and brevity.

You'll find endnotes and three appendices at the back of the book. I believe avoiding footnotes makes for an easier read of material that is already fraught with speed bumps and potholes.

My healing journey has been long and difficult but very worthwhile. I am not the same shattered person I was when the journey began. And if God could do all this for me, He can certainly do this for you or someone you know. He only asks for cooperation in the process. He yearns for you to seek His help.

May God fill you with His love and grace, for these are His tools for healing.

Introduction

A word of caution: if any of the material in this book triggers you, don't try to work through it by yourself. Contact a counselor or minister experienced in working with dissociative clients.

1

Discovery

July 1999

I woke in the pitch dark of my bedroom. No telling what time it was. My mind, paralyzed by fear, refused all attempts at analysis.

I couldn't swallow, couldn't even breathe. Instinctively, I rolled out of bed and crouched on all fours, allowing saliva to drain. It was either that or risk choking on it. I fought hard to inhale, but my lungs refused all efforts at expansion.

No air moved.

I staggered into the bathroom. My hand groped for the light switch. The sudden brightness temporarily blinded me, but the painful glare managed to relieve some fear. I would survive. I wouldn't die alone in the dark, without a soul to know exactly what had happened.

Slowly, air began to flow into my tortured lungs again. My heart slowed. Panic eased.

Death would not claim me this night.

Terrifying nocturnal episodes continued all week. I worried my work might be suffering from my lack of sleep. This might not be such a problem with some other jobs, but patients depended on my decision-making skills as a physician assistant. Fear and fatigue could be a dangerous combination. I had to get help.

My primary doctor couldn't tell me exactly what was happening to me, but he did know what it wasn't. Not asthma, not acid reflux and choking, not thyroid swelling. But simply admitting my paralyzing fear to him helped smooth my jagged emotions.

Seeing the unshed tears glinting in my eyes, he gently laid a hand on my shoulder and spoke in a soft and confident tone: "I know this must be really scary. We'll get it figured out." His compassion reassured me I wasn't losing my mind.

He referred me to a pulmonologist for further evaluation.

Anxiety ridden, I waited for my scheduled appointment and breathed a sigh of relief when it finally arrived after about a week. Maybe now I could get an answer.

The lung specialist listened to my story and then performed a brief exam. The final test was of my gag reflex. She wrapped a piece of gauze around her finger and thumb and then tugged on my tongue. I nearly gagged up my socks. She jumped back, perhaps protecting her shoes, before declaring, "That's quite an active reflex you've got there."

Once I'd recovered from my near-violent response, she proclaimed the diagnosis: severe vocal cord dysfunction (VCD).

I shook my head. "Uh, okay. What's that?" Twelve years practicing as a physician assistant (PA) in internal medicine and three years as an ambulance emergency medical technician (EMT) and still I'd never heard of this condition. Dr.

Chang showed me a diagram and explained the reason for my symptoms. Fear gradually gave way to curiosity. This was getting interesting, even though it was happening to me.

The doctor pointed to the illustration of vocal cords during an attack. Sail shaped, the vocal cords joined virtually completely, leaving only a straw-size opening at one end to breathe through. Bad enough, but the topper was when she showed me how the membranes tightened against the pressure of inhaling. No wonder I was so terrified!

The doctor explained further as she ticked off her fingers for each point. "These are the most common characteristics of someone who develops VCD: female, late thirties and forties, professional, perfectionistic, tends to repress emotion. Does any of that fit you?"

I was stunned—and chagrined. I nodded reluctantly. "All of the above."

Dr. Chang's face held a sympathetic smile. "All right. Here's what we need to do now: I'm referring you to a speech therapist. Deanna will teach you how to control the physical symptoms, not only to terminate the attacks but to prevent them from developing."

Nodding, I tucked Deanna's business card into my jeans pocket.

"Severe vocal cord dysfunction is very often associated with a history of sexual abuse," she continued. "Any knowledge of something like that?"

I had a few conscious memories of being sexually harassed by an older neighbor boy when I was around eleven. Not a big deal, I thought.

I'd gone to his house to hang out with his sisters. When I headed to the gate to leave, he pulled his now-usual trick. "You can't leave until you give me a kiss."

I glared at him. "Get out of my way."

He grinned and stepped closer.

I'd finally had enough. I took off my dressy shoe, held it up, and warned him what would happen. He laughed, so I hit his thigh with my half-inch stack heel. That stopped his obnoxious behavior for good.

But lately, some haunting memories and flashes of images had been invading my body and my mind. I told the doctor everything I could think of. It wasn't much. Afterward, I fell silent.

"This is all a manifestation of post-traumatic stress disorder. Most people know about PTSD associated with combat veterans, but it's pretty common with rape victims as well as with childhood sexual abuse."

I gasped as my heart pounded. Was she kidding? Rape? Sexual abuse? Nothing like that had ever happened . . . had it?

"I strongly recommend you start therapy. I'd be happy to refer you to the Mental Health Department."

Whoa! Stop right there! No way was I going to have a mental health referral and diagnosis and visit notes in my chart. I had to work with these people. If anyone found out . . .

"No, thanks. I know someone. I'll give her a call."

"As soon as you can. This is important."

I left the doctor's office feeling a bit of relief over the vocal cord dysfunction. This was a medical problem—familiar territory. I could deal with that, but the PTSD stuff was a different animal altogether.

Now I had the fear of the unknown added to the fear of nighttime attacks. The resulting anxiety constantly gnawed at the edges of my consciousness. I jumped at any sudden noises. Anxiety took aim at my appetite. Fatigue made me drag all day. Any tension, even a slightly dry throat, and my voice stopped. I learned to always keep a lozenge in my pocket. Thank God for my current graduate-level PA student, who took over when I could no longer speak.

I feared being found on the clinic floor, unconscious from an attack. A physician colleague reassured me that if I passed out, the muscles would relax and breathing would resume automatically. Whew!

Remarkably, as time passed, so did the nocturnal VCD attacks. The few that occurred during daytime hours faded more slowly, but full-blown episodes became merely a memory within a few weeks. I don't really know why. I suspect working with Deanna (speech therapist extraordinaire) helped more than I knew.

The first thing she taught me was to exhale gently to help the membranes and muscles relax. Completely counterintuitive, but there it was. Once I knew I could abort an episode, my stress level decreased markedly.

I remember being in the back yard, mowing the lawn, when an attack started a couple of weeks later.

Panic didn't hit me quite as hard this time.

My neck muscles tightened. I started coughing. Soon I whooped and gasped for air. I went to my knees and practiced what Deanna had taught me. The attack eased.

A few minutes later I was sitting indoors on my stairway, drinking some water. My next-door neighbor came to the front door. Seeing me there, he asked, "Hey, are you all right?"

"Oh, yeah. Had a cough, so I came in for some water."

He didn't quite believe my answer, so he asked again, "Are you sure you're all right? I saw you go down."

After receiving a few more details about my condition, he said, "Take care of yourself. If you need anything, just call. You've got our number, right?"

I did. And I would.

As I'd promised Dr. Chang, I called right away for a counseling appointment. I'd seen Phoebe for some minor issues in the past. This time my call wasn't nearly so casual.

Waiting for my appointment with Phoebe seemed an eternity though it was only a few weeks. Later I discovered she'd bumped me to the top of her long waiting list; she'd felt God's urgency about my situation. Clearly, somebody had been praying for me—I certainly didn't have any faith for myself right then.

My first appointment was unremarkable. I filled out some forms. Phoebe and I discussed what had been happening to me. We prayed together for wisdom and guidance. Then Phoebe sent me home with the reassurance that someone cared and, more important, understood.

Oh, but the second visit! After a few minutes, Phoebe looked me straight in the eyes and asked, "Do you realize you're dissociative?"

I frowned at her, confused and ignorant. "Huh?"

Then she explained the term as I listened in disbelief. "Basically, a young mind doesn't have the ability to deal with traumatic events—the child hasn't learned logical thinking and reasoning. So, to handle the trauma, most of the mind turns away from seeing, feeling, and hearing it while another, small part absorbs the pain. This 'little one' stays stuck in the memory and guards it against discovery. And it all remains hidden until something happens to bring it to our attention, like your vocal cord issues."

That took some pondering. I, of course, not only had no idea about my own dissociation, but no concept of the implications.

But now it was time to choose: go forward with God and a trusted counselor or stay stuck in my dysfunction and pain.

That day I began my journey through the darkness of a dissociative disorder—the exploration, revelation, and gradual healing from the effects of trauma-based mind control.

PAIN

Pain is, at first, just an unexpected guest.
Soon it overstays its welcome,
develops roots, and grows.
Eventually you get used to the intruder
and just bear it.
You find ways to remove yourself
because there is no way to remove it.
Other people see the removed you
and assume all is well.
They don't see the barrier
holding them at arm's length,
the barrier preventing them from giving you more pain,
more than you have now,
more than you can bear.
Sometimes you let someone in.
Someone who seems trustworthy,
Who acts concerned
Who will not judge
And life seems better . . .
Until they bring you more pain,
pain you knew not to allow,
and it continues.
You know somewhere out there is a person or persons
holding the key to your release.
You hope they will find you,
hope they will not be fooled by your barrier,
hope they will rescue you from exile
because you know you can't do it yourself.
All your strength is used up by
living with the pain.

2

Fear

The more Phoebe explained the basics of dissociation,[1] the more my past and present issues and oddities began to make a kind of sense:

The gaps in my childhood memory that continue to annoy me. When I look back, my memory is full of holes, like Swiss cheese. I don't know what I don't know.

The knowledge I utilized without any memory of having learned it. For example, my dorm mates in college often asked me for boyfriend advice. Then they followed my recommendations, and no one ever asked, "What were you thinking?!"

What was up with that? I'd never had a boyfriend, so I attributed my advice to simple logic. Some of it probably was, but what about the rest?

The strange dreams, complete with strong physical and sexual sensations.

The magnetic draw of pornography and sex at a very young and innocent age.

The terrifying nocturnal episodes when I woke in a panic, fully conscious but knowing an evil presence was in my bedroom. I never had any memory of a dream and recalled these episodes the next morning and beyond.

The irrational creepiness of some seemingly innocuous objects or images, like the peeling skin of a cooking lima bean or the surface fragmentation of dried mud. Worse yet, someone peeling off sunburned skin—ew! But why didn't a sloughed snakeskin set me off?

My peculiarities kept piling up:

The hypervigilance that made me cringe when loud noises or flashes of light startled me: a sudden crash from a waiter's dropped glass invariably triggered long moments of heart racing and internal tremors. Why didn't my companions ever react the way I did? I could never understand how they stayed so calm.

Even now, the hypersensitive vestiges of PTSD remain. They're not as intense, but the raucous clang from a dropped weight at the gym just grinds on me. I still jump at the sudden noise.

My discomfort with Halloween and the inordinate fear of going to a "haunted house." When I was a high school junior, my friends convinced me to go to one with them. It was supposed to be good, scary fun. The resulting nightmares recurred for many years. And they were never about the displays of monsters and ghosts. No, just crawling through the dark tunnel into the house had terrified me. Of course, I never let on to my friends.

While in my forties and visiting a counselor friend in Ohio, I freaked out from going into a bookstore elaborately decorated for Halloween. We started exploring the section that sold witchy stuff, and I practically ran out, heart racing, until Tom calmed me down. And by the way, corn mazes? Uh-uh.

Full moons, especially those occurring on Halloween, unsettled me even if I wasn't aware of them.

Fear

The apprehension of going into someone else's home. I turned down lots of invitations over the years that I know now were genuine expressions of friendship. When I did reluctantly accept, I was almost always on high alert when entering an unfamiliar space, even if I knew who would be there. Taking the "grand tour" of someone's house—out of the question! All I wanted was to finish the tour and get to a safe place.

Even more fearsome than entering another's home was the thought of eating there. And the whole thing also worked in reverse—inviting someone into my place was nerve-racking, so it rarely happened. When it did, I never had more than two or three people over at a time, and I had to know them really well. They had to be benign enough for me to feel safe in my sanctuary.

What about the lack of emotional depth? I didn't think anyone knew about my inability to feel deeply. I lost that self-deception during a college class discussion about the poetry of Emily Dickinson. I decided to offer my opinion of her work, starting with, "I feel like . . ." Then a classmate interrupted me, declaring for all to hear, "You don't have any feelings!"

I didn't feel anything? Anything at all?

Of course, I felt stuff. I wasn't a robot. I didn't feel anything strongly, and I just never reacted like other girls. But I did feel happy with Christmas presents, satisfaction from getting good grades, and amusement at kitten antics. I felt sadness when I broke my long-eared doggy bank, anger at being harassed by a neighbor boy, and frustration at missing an easy math question.

But underneath it all lurked something else. Something huge.

That something was fear.

Although I believe people generally thought me courageous once I reached adolescence, no one knew it was all bluff and bluster. The only time this pseudo-bravery surfaced was when I was in control and in a safe place. Generally, this meant an intellectual setting, where facts reigned. Emotions confused and frightened me. I commonly isolated for self-protection. I'm an introvert, yes, but this went much further. And it wasn't just physical, but emotional and mental.

As long as I could think clearly, I could reason my way out of a bad situation. Self-control was paramount. *Star Trek*'s Mr. Spock became more than just an interesting character. His personality suited me just fine. Logic had kept me safe, too.

I feared everything and everyone I couldn't control.

Fear remained the one constant in my life—my primary motivator. I hated being at parties and receptions, despised social small talk. Until recently I hadn't a clue how to act or what to say without fear of appearing a fool. I wondered how in the world all those other people knew how to act. Why did it seem instinctual for them?

I despised myself for feeling weak and out of control while secretly envying and loathing those who moved through society with ease. Quiet corners away from the crowd helped me retain some sanity until I could leave without offending the hosts. I learned to say upon my arrival at an event, "I can only stay for a little while."

Fear kept me from dating. I always told myself that guys were just people. It didn't help. Once a boy I knew from high school drama class dropped by on a Saturday evening to ask me to a movie. I hid in the kitchen. Wouldn't even go into the living room to talk to him. The poor guy could see me, though, as I declared I had to help Mom with the dishes. She quietly gave me her permission to leave, but fear held my feet to the floor. I later learned my father had finally suggested the boy go on home. Needless to say, he never asked me out again.

Fear of failure became a self-fulfilling prophecy. It kept me from holding on to any full-time job longer than six months until I became a physician assistant (PA) in my thirties. Until then I'd spent a lot of time working for a temporary agency. There was safety in that lack of commitment. As long as the work gets done, nobody really notices a temp.

Although my ambitions were pretty high, deep-seated fear kept me from making any goals that might prove too challenging. I believed in my own intelligence and skills but not in efforts toward unknown heights. No big risks for this girl! It wouldn't be safe.

Earning a college undergraduate degree in biology/chemistry, training as an emergency medical technician (EMT) and working as an ambulance attendant, graduating from a highly regarded physician assistant program and practicing medicine—these were actually comparatively safe endeavors. Those challenges were to my mind, not my heart. I could handle that.

Fear prevented me from forming truly close friendships. (Honestly, I didn't understand what would constitute a close friendship.) What if someone found out about the real me? Even I didn't know that much about me.

Once, while in my early thirties, I was pointed out as an example of integrity—being the same on the outside as on the inside. No, the discussion leader wasn't seeing integrity. This was my own ignorance of what existed within me mixed with fear of doing something to elicit disapproval, especially from God and His representatives.

I rose to a second-level leadership position at my large church's singles' group. That earned me a measure of respect and helped me feel a bit better about myself. I didn't realize it at the time, but being in charge without being too high up the ladder kept me feeling safe from attack, no matter where it might come from.

People seemed to listen when I spoke, and they often quieted when I entered a noisy room. I didn't learn until recently that I had carried an air of spiritual authority as a result of fighting and surviving my abusive history.

Many children turn to Jesus when they realize God's love for them. Not me. Fear of death made me do it.

I was ten or eleven when I went to a children's crusade at the church I'd been attending with neighbor kids. The guest ministers held a nightly marionette show during the weeklong crusade. That night they told the Exodus story of the Passover—and the death angel terrified me. I was literally scared into the kingdom of God.

When I later started hearing stories of people being drawn or even overcome by God's love, I wondered, *Why not me?*

I asked my pastor about this several years ago. He knew my background, so I figured he might have an answer. What Don had was a question. "Do you think you would have been able to accept God's love back then?"

I had to admit I wouldn't have.

"Then that was His love. It was the only way He could reach you."

Although I didn't particularly like it, that answer made sense.

Other people didn't seem to be afraid all the time. I never understood why I was. I believe the fear made me a target for the harassment and bullying that started early on.

One day while a friend and I were walking to elementary school, a younger neighbor boy blocked our path. He told us we had to pay a toll or we couldn't pass. I burst into tears, desperately worried about being late.

"Gee, I was only kidding!" he said, his disgust evident.

But my friend stood up to his challenge. In a voice that left no room for doubt, she told him, "Get out of our way!"

I, for whatever reason, took his threat as real. And I cowered before a small child playing a pirate's bluff.

My biggest fear was of rejection and abandonment. I constantly subjugated my own desires so I wouldn't be rejected for being "different." A lot of good that did. It only increased my invisibility.

I denied, even to myself, that my needs existed. Asking for help was tantamount to admitting inadequacy and defeat.

With lots of practice and hard work, I got pretty good at faking happy involvement while absolutely believing my lot in life was to be alone and unwanted. No effort from others or my own mind could convince me otherwise. I tried to find healing with several counselors over a decade. Antidepressants and talk therapy never had a positive effect on me, and certainly no lasting change occurred.

As a college freshman, I was required to have an introductory session with a counselor. The head of that department went over my standardized test scores, and we discussed my life and goals. Wrapping it up, he told me I was normal, just "an average, lonely freshman."

He didn't know the half of it!

The diagnosis of dissociative identity disorder gave me a few answers about my lifelong pain and fear. Unfortunately, healing wasn't nearly so rapid.

One of the early session notes illustrates my internal landscape. Walking through darkness, isolated from others, seeing their happiness and enjoyment of life, made me feel as if I were living under an eternal curse of hopelessness.

The mental video played:

Adult persona: I see a little one who's trying to hold a wall together, but she can't control it anymore. It's all she can pay attention to. Finally, she agrees to let Jesus help as long as nobody finds out she's not doing her job anymore.

Little one speaking: *We still have to look behind the wall, but it would be okay because I don't have to do it anymore 'cause He's in charge. I don't want to look but I think it will be okay. He's big and strong.*

John: Well, Lord Jesus, let's look behind the wall. Is that okay?

Little one: *I want to be farther away. I don't want it to spill on me when it comes out.*

(momentary silence)

John: What's going on?

Little one: *He opened it up and we went inside. It's dark, and it feels thick, like walking through water maybe.*

This is weird. I see a bank vault. It's a detour. I feel like I'm supposed to turn to the right and keep going.

Fear

The farther I go, the more I'm alone and the more fear there is. It feels like there's no end to the darkness.

I see places on the sides that are light but I can't go there. I have to stay in the dark. It's just where I have to be. I see some of the light places have people in them and they're having fun and are happy and it's like, "I don't belong with them. It's not for me." I have to stay in the dark, in the center, and we have to keep going.

Now I'm hearing some voices from the outside. They're saying "Don't look to the right or the left. This is your path. Walk in it."

Admittedly, variations on the theme of abandonment abound, and everyone has experienced rejection at some point in life. So what had happened to me?

What could have caused this depth of pain and intensity of fear? The truth was eventually unearthed from deep within my own mind. "Little ones," dissociated parts of my mind, worked hard to guard and hide a myriad of memories, not releasing them until they were discovered and encouraged to do so by Jesus.

To live in constant fear is to be in prison. But when you know nothing except the prison, it seems like home. It feels normal. Fear and ignorance keep you from seeking escape. That is, until something makes escape seem preferable.

And maybe, just maybe . . . possible.

SHAME

Shame covers me
Like an old wool coat.
Heavy, rough, it even smells musty.
It doesn't let me breathe . . .
I can't get out from under it.

I let them do it. Nothing can ever change that.
There is no hope . . . I can't get rid of it.
Nothing I do will ever wash it clean.
There's no power that can change it.
Even Jesus won't accept me now.

But then I see Him . . . beaten,
Jeered and leered at, spat on . . .
Shamed deeply.

He was innocent . . . but so was I.
I let them do it . . . so did He.
He was shamed . . . so was I.
But He let them shame Him
So my shame could be taken away.
The shame belongs to those who hurt Him,
And to those who hurt me.
Just as it does not belong to Him,
It does not belong to me.
And it does not belong to you. Never did.
Let it go.

3

Shame

Other than fear, the only emotion I consistently felt was shame. This followed me well into the healing journey.

Apparently, the shame began before I developed any conscious memories. Of course, I didn't know it by that name. What I did know was that something was terribly wrong with me and I didn't belong anywhere.

I always felt guilty and as if I deserved punishment, though I could rarely point to a specific wrongdoing. My mom told me I was a very easy child, that she could always expect me to do the right thing. I so rarely got in trouble (unlike my older siblings) that I clearly remember the times I did. Usually, if I did get in trouble, it was because I had made a sarcastic, smart-aleck remark and refused to repeat it. That earned me a swat on the behind and the order "Go to your room!"

Having such tight self-imposed limits is a miserable way to live. You're always trying to be perfect. And you never allow yourself to truly be a kid.

No freedom, no joy exists in it. Always guilty, always full of shame.

During the long healing journey, I learned that *guilt* is a legal term. It's recognition that you've broken a rule and done something legally wrong. Some penalty must be paid, but then you are exonerated. There is hope for redemption.

Shame in its original godly sense is simply an emotional realization and acknowledgment that you've done something to damage a relationship, that you *did* something morally wrong.

Sadly, the enemy of our souls has honed shame to a fine point until it's become destructive. Shame in this sense is a pervasive feeling and knowledge (though false) that you *are* something wrong.

You feel you are guilty of whatever accusations are leveled at you.

What about that damaged relationship? No matter what you do or say, you know nothing will repair it. You are doomed forever to be an outsider.

There is no hope for redemption. Not for you.

This includes the relationship with yourself, as in self-hatred. You hate yourself for who you are. You believe without a doubt that no one genuinely loves or even likes you. You are damaged goods. And you have no idea why.

It just . . . is.

I have yet to see an abuse survivor who doesn't wrestle with this distorted type of shame. This emotion paralyzes you. It makes you feel as though everything that happened was somehow your fault.

That was what I felt. That was how I lived.

We know that a child cannot do anything to deserve sexual molestation or rape. Childish misbehavior does not invite beatings and bruises or worse. But somehow, when it's our own problem, we can't see the truth. Shame becomes our (false) identity.

Shame

It was mine for many years.

You've likely heard the term *performance oriented*. This alignment is one hallmark of a shame-based person. Performance-oriented people can't fail—that's unacceptable. Unfortunately, we fear success as much as we do failure. You see, a success demands increased future effort. It sets the achievement bar higher. And if we try to reach that new level, the odds shift and make us feel even likelier to fail sometime, somewhere. When the inevitable failure occurs, we feel even more unacceptable.

So where did all my shame come from? And why couldn't I recognize it for what it was?

The brutal truth was, I had been subjected to *trauma-based mind control* (TBMC) at a very young age. Some people call it *ritual abuse* (RA).[2] It has been called *satanic ritual abuse* (SRA) for the simple reason that it is satanically inspired. Whatever phrase is used, I'd grown up with dissociation as a result. In the most basic terms, I had major gaps in my memories because they had been separated from my conscious mind by repeated trauma. Those gaps held the little ones, who guarded the painful memories against discovery.

After Phoebe broached the subject of dissociation, I had tons of questions. Fortunately, tons of answers also awaited discovery. Phoebe explained the *how* first.

"I'm sure you know the established responses to fear: fight or flight. And the most recent addition: freeze."

I nodded. Learned that in college—basic psychology. These instinctive responses protected animals and people in dangerous situations.

Then Phoebe shared something we hadn't learned in Psych 101: "But a child who is being traumatized only has three ways to escape. She can die physically since she's too small to fight successfully. Or she can die mentally by going insane since she's too young to reason logically. Or she can retreat into herself by dissociating. You chose to dissociate. And it saved you."

"You mean I'm not just crazy? Not funny farm material?"

Phoebe chuckled at my bid for humor. "No, not crazy. Just badly wounded. And very strong. Only strong children survive these ordeals essentially intact. Fragile kids are rarely exploited because they simply won't make it. We're talking about mental capability and intelligence, and emotional as well as physical power. That combined strength is imperative if someone is to learn survival through dissociation.

"If a child isn't forced into learning how to dissociate at a young age—some say by four years of age, others by six—chances are dissociation won't be learned. Not to the extent of a lifelong issue, at least, and not as an automatic response. And, might I add, although it's considered a mental illness, it's actually a God-given aid to the defenseless."

Since I was ignorant on the subject, except for what Phoebe explained, I had no response. Of course, later I had to spend a long time pondering and testing the premise, but for now, Phoebe's explanation was enough.

I chose to trust her.

Then I spent the next thirty months learning the effects dissociation had had on my life.

Phoebe and I processed (with God's help) memory after painful memory. We generally started with the most recent issues and went backward chronologically. We didn't choose that method; it was simply how God orchestrated it.

I believe now that He started with the less traumatic memories (conscious as well as repressed) and then progressed to deeper and more intense ones as I grew in knowledge and received healing. His mercy would not allow me to be overwhelmed.

I learned that God truly exists outside of time—He is omnitemporal, if you will. He knows the end from the beginning (see Isaiah 46:10) and dwells in all of it. He can go back into your past, reveal the source of pain, and heal it. He speaks truth to the lies you now believe and to the lies you've lived with your entire life. He meant it when He said, "The truth will set you free" (John 8:32 NIV).

God's healing also affects your present and your future. Of course, healing doesn't mean God will change the memory—what happened to you is a historical fact. Any therapy or theory that says you can change the facts of the trauma according to your own desire is in error. You can't wish this away.

I also learned that my pain wasn't only from what had actually happened in my life, but also from my reaction to it. I had undoubtedly believed lies about myself since I was a toddler. Some were actually forced on me by my perpetrators; some I absorbed from my surroundings. And some were false conclusions from my own confused, hurt, and angry mind.

The strongest, most common, and most pervasive lie? *You are alone and helpless.* That was actually true, but only in the basic physical sense. God was always with me. Of course, the most believable lies have a grain of truth in them.

A close second? *You are worthless, and you deserve whatever happened to you.* I believed that even though God loves everybody, He could never love me. How could He possibly love me if He let all this bad stuff happen? If I deserved it? If I was bad? Even unredeemable?

And the ultimate conclusion: *If even God can't love me, I am completely unlovable.*

See the circular thinking? It starts with an occurrence: *Bad stuff is happening.*

Then it goes to a question: *How could God let this happen?*

Then a lie: *He doesn't love me.*

Then more lies: *I must be unlovable. I am worthless. It's all my fault.*

And the lies pile on top of one another until a child is confused and lost in them. No person can tell her the truth—her mind simply cannot accept it.

But God bypasses the mind and speaks truth to the heart. A traumatized, dissociative grown-up "child" can receive His truth, but she usually needs someone to help her and to teach her how. Chances are good that she's heard too many voices in her head for too long a time to discern the sources. These are usually voices from dissociated parts but can also be from the evil one or from God. The result? Confusion.

During my time with Phoebe, I also learned just how extensive my dissociation was. One day at work, I entered the exam room to see my first patient of the afternoon. Her tall and husky husband accompanied her and sat in the second chair between me and the door.

I'd never seen this patient before, so I asked questions about her history. The conversation went something like this:

> **Me**: I'm going to list your medications and you tell me if you're still taking each one, okay?
>
> **Her**: All right.

Shame

When I noticed her antianxiety med had not been refilled recently, I told her what I saw and asked, "Are you still taking this one?"

Her: Of course I am! I always take them like I'm supposed to!

Me: Okay. I just needed to check.

Her: You're not my doctor. I didn't want to see you, anyway! She never says I'm crazy. She likes me! You're calling me crazy, and I'm not crazy! I'm sick of it! Sick of you!

I had done no such thing—hadn't decided anything about her at all. I was just gathering basic information.

Her evident agitation escalated. She fidgeted on the exam table, bouncing her foot and glancing around the room. No eye contact. And I wasn't about to force it.

Her: I don't have to sit here and take this!

She stormed out into the hall. Should I call security?
Her husband spoke: "Maybe I should go after her."
I agreed.
After he had calmed her down, both the husband and his wife returned to the exam room and resumed their places. The appointment proceeded normally. I went back to my office to chart the visit before my next patient arrived.
The next thing I remember, I was preparing to go home. I straightened up my desk and put the day's charts into my outbox to be distributed to the doctors. Then I glanced at

my wristwatch. Five o'clock? Where had the time gone? How had I lost an entire afternoon?

Phoebe and I discussed it the next day. She understood and explained the virtually predictable sequence:

- A perceived threat from the patient caused fear.
- Fear made me dissociate.
- My dissociated state erased my perception of passing time.

Weird. But it finally made sense. Dissociated parts (or "little ones") dwelled in my mind. They protected me from perceived threats. At least one was sufficiently mature and knew my job well enough that she could take over my actions while I watched from a mentally and emotionally safe place. Most likely I had given her directions from the sidelines. All was well.

This dissociative incident was the longest one I experienced after my diagnosis. Most were momentary or entailed only partial dissociation. Often my vision would blur a bit as though I looked through panes of dirty glass. Or I would feel distant from myself, but still aware and in control.

After we'd worked together for a few months, Phoebe described the continuum of dissociation. "Think of it as a yardstick that runs from one to one hundred. The single digits symbolize people with a normal level of dissociation." She explained that everyone takes "mind vacations" because the mind gets bored with repetitive activities, like driving a familiar stretch of highway or while mowing the lawn. Part of the mind finishes the task while the rest zones out, returning to attention when life gets more interesting.

"The higher numbers correlate to deeper, more complex levels of dissociation. You're up there in the higher ranges, but not as bad as it could be. Problematic, but not a huge problem." Phoebe had recently completed an advanced internship on working with dissociation, so she spoke with earned authority. However, that initial evaluation eventually proved to be woefully inadequate.

I worked diligently with Phoebe, learning, processing memories, and healing. During that time, we discovered significantly more about why I'd developed dissociation.

Since we didn't know what had happened or who the perpetrators were, we had to lean on God to reveal the truth. Phoebe did have her suspicions.

Before I left one day, she handed me a small paperback book titled *Free from Freemasonry*.[3] "Read this and put a sticky note on every page that triggers you," she said. "Keep it as long as you need to."

"Okay. I can do that."

Before I go any further with this, allow me to explain triggering.

At its most basic, a *trigger response* is a disproportionate reaction to rather normal occurrences. It's more than a simple heads-up. It goes deeper than the mind. When I got triggered, I felt sudden revulsion and fear, even panic. My stomach tightened and I often got nauseated. My palms might sweat. My vision got fuzzy around the edges, sometimes to the point of tunnel vision.

A trigger causes an adrenaline rush for no apparent reason. Sensations assault the body. Often a flash of an image arises. What you are actually seeing or hearing rarely correlates with your present experiences. The specifics are different for everyone. And an individual can experience different types of reactions—physical, emotional, mental—depending on the trigger and its source.

My Personal Holocaust

As an example, one of my early triggers involved a 1992 Mel Gibson movie, *Forever Young*. I was watching it on television one Sunday evening. The main character was a mid-twentieth-century man who had been cryogenically frozen for decades at midlife and then awakened in an unfamiliar time. When I saw the khaki pants snugged to his waist by a brown leather belt, alarm bells went off in my head.

I jumped out of my chair and ran upstairs. Trembling with a fear I couldn't shake, I called a trusted friend.

"I'm even having trouble breathing. All this over a movie? That's crazy!"

My friend's calm voice filtered through the phone. "Sounds like you're having a body memory. You know, when the body remembers what the mind forgot. You've definitely been triggered."

"Well, what am I supposed to do about it? It's Sunday night, for Pete's sake!"

"I know this might sound silly, but start cleaning your kitchen or something. Get your mind occupied with other details. Put on some worship music. And tell Phoebe about it soon. This has to be from a buried memory."

So, at my next session with Phoebe, we explored the incident. Sure enough, following the fear led to a memory of alcohol-fueled molestation by a neighbor. The man had had a bottle of whiskey out on his enclosed back porch. I was a small and curious child. The rest followed.

I kept the book Phoebe had assigned to me for several weeks; I trusted her even though I had no clue where she was going with the assignment. I did my homework, got triggered in the process, and put a sticky note (or two) on that page.

Seeing a picture or description in there that triggered me didn't just affect my mind and body. No, it shook my very soul. And I didn't know why.

That was always the worst—not knowing why something triggered me. Why would an old photograph and description of a cave where Masonic ceremonies were held make my inner landscape shake like a 7.5 Richter earthquake?

Why would a picture of a repulsive two-headed, mixed-gender, goatlike demonic image draw me with such fascination that I couldn't make myself look away?

When seeing a whirlpool-like vortex (even a simple hand-drawn one), why did I feel myself being sucked into it? Why did it give me tunnel vision and produce queasiness?

Just what had happened to cause all this emotional damage? Did I need to know? And more important, did I want to?

I had to keep reading. And rereading.

4

Transitions

I had started meeting with my counselor, Phoebe, in late August 1999. She gave me *Free from Freemasonry* in late October.

By the time January 2000 rolled around, the poor little paperback book Phoebe had given me sported what looked a batch of two-inch-square yellow feathers. And the sticky notes were not just here and there, but all around the edges—and all the way through the text. Kind of like Big Bird, but not nearly so innocuous.

"Here you go." I handed Phoebe the book before I took my usual seat on the office couch across from her rocker. I tucked a foot under me and mentally prepared for the session. "That was . . . interesting."

Phoebe rocked slowly in her chair as she flipped through the pages. "Wow. There are a lot of places marked here."

"I was careful. I only marked the stuff I was sure about." I didn't want her to think I'd faked it.

"No, no, I understand," she said, looking at me. She lowered her gaze back to the book, following the trail of my sticky notes. Then she sighed. "This answers a lot of our questions."

"Oh?"

"I'd say you were traumatized by some Masonic group when you were very young."

"But no one in my family was into that!" I said. "What I know about Masons would fit in a teaspoon. Besides, there's no Masonic stuff in our house—I'm sure I would have known about it. And I've never seen anything like what was in the pictures in that book. Well, sure, I've seen caves and old buildings and monuments, but they never made me freak out! I mean, I love historical places, even cemeteries—"

Phoebe's calm, measured voice broke through my confusion and rising alarm. "Hey, slow down. Take a breath." She paused, waiting for me to refocus. "The dissociation and triggering aren't from just seeing the historical places; it's from the spiritual darkness that inhabits those places. And that comes from the ceremonies that have happened there."

My memory flashed to something my close friend Linda had said to me shortly before I started seeing Phoebe: "I'll bet you're Masonic."

I'd pooh-poohed that and then packed it neatly into the furthest storage bin in my mind. Linda's statement simply made no sense. And after saying it once more, Linda had dropped the subject until I'd been in counseling for a year or so. Then she gradually revealed that her father had been an active member of the Buffalo lodge and she had been traumatized by his group. I didn't feel quite so alone after that. What I'd thought was rare or even isolated, wasn't—not at all.

I learned that between 1 percent and 3 percent of the US population may be survivors of trauma-based mind control, from whatever source. This estimate is not entirely accurate because so many survivors have not yet reached the point of experiencing PTSD symptoms or discovering repressed memories. It could be significantly higher. As it is, the total is a mind-numbing 6.6 million people.

At least two-thirds of these are women. Subjects are chosen between the ages of eighteen and twenty-four months because this is the time when children differentiate, that is, when the child begins to see herself as a separate individual from the mother. This is also when personality development occurs.

The cults tend to choose girls for several reasons: girls mature faster than boys, both physically and mentally. They tend to be more pliable. And cults that are ruled by demonic forces are misogynistic (characterized by hatred of women). This is because Satan hates and fears women. The curses uttered by God in Genesis 3 are clear: Eve's anger would forever be focused on Satan, and the seed of the woman—Jesus—would defeat him.[4] Yes, Satan has already been defeated, but he's still fighting for all he's worth.

After about two years of our working together, Phoebe sensed the Lord asking her to give up her practice and to devote more time to teaching overseas. I know now she dreaded the thought of leaving her clients dangling.

My heart ached, feeling abandoned at receiving a letter from her.

"That's it?" I demanded. "You send a form letter to give me the bad news?"

"No, I made each letter individual, just like each of you." Phoebe sighed. "I was afraid of this reaction. I just didn't know how to soften it. I'm sorry."

Phoebe and I only had a little while before her practice was to close; we did as much as we could in the intervening weeks and months. She copied a seven-page Masonic renunciation prayer so we could break the curses Masons call down on themselves and their descendants through the vows they utter.

A year later I discovered a comparison of Masonic vows printed in parallel with those taken by witches' covens. The Masonic vows actually submitted the participant to more severe potential violence and bloodletting if they ever revealed any secrets of the lodge. The Masonic vows also declared their oaths to be in effect in perpetuity... throughout their generations.

One wonders if the Masons truly understand what they are doing and saying. Admittedly, the consequences tend not to be exactly the same as the words, but, for example, a vow about having the bowels torn out can manifest symbolically as colon cancer or some other issue requiring abdominal surgery. The cause is this: Masons curse themselves and their descendants without grasping the significance of their words.

And here's the deeply frightening part: the words the participants speak as vows can seem melodramatic, even silly, like having "the left breast torn open and the heart plucked out and given to the fowls of the air" (Second Degree, Fellow Craft—an introductory level). Masons also vow to "aid and assist a companion Freemason when engaged in any difficulty, whether he be right or wrong, murder or treason not excepted" (Royal Arch Degree, York Rite—a high level).[5]

Melodramatic, yes, but the spirit world takes them seriously. So does a child who hears these terrifying declarations.

Working with Phoebe, I'd processed memories of sexual molestation by a neighbor and by my grandfather. We'd discovered a buried memory of rape by a stranger, which added credence to the physical evidence that my first period was actually a miscarriage. And we had dealt with my very first conscious memory: when I fell down the stairs at my parents' new house into the basement and landed on the back of my head on the concrete floor. I always thought this was a dream, but Mom tells me it actually happened. She was terrified that I'd been killed because I didn't cry or respond to her voice. But I never fully lost consciousness.

Phoebe and I had to seek out the lies I'd believed about this painful fall as a three-year-old. In the memory, I felt as though I had purposefully thrown myself down the stairs and into the dark basement. Had I actually wanted to die at that moment?

Jesus faithfully helped me heal as we dealt with a bunch of freaky and frightening stuff.

We also discovered things that should have been less traumatizing but were augmented by earlier, even more terrifying incidents. I remember seeing a real-life example of this when our ambulance crew was on standby at a city fireworks display. A bottle rocket landed in a crate of unused fireworks and set them all off in a huge explosion. A man fell, wounded. One of our officers threw himself over him. This posttraumatic flashback caused the officer to literally relive a battle, complete with sights, sounds, smells, and emotions.

Soon the closing of Phoebe's practice loomed. We knew we had processed an ocean's worth of the more surface issues, but we also knew it was all preliminary to the main event. I had to go much deeper; I still had to deal with the results of ritual abuse. Had to face what had happened, work through it, and allow God to heal.

I didn't want to lose momentum, but quitting would be so easy right now.

Phoebe was leaving me. How could I continue the work without a counselor who knew what to do? I couldn't stop now. I needed someone who could hear from God and help me do the same, someone who had seen this sort of thing before. Someone who wouldn't think I was nuts. Who wouldn't judge me. Another woman who would understand just how defiled and broken I was and still not give up on me.

Just how was I supposed to find her? Phoebe gave one suggestion, but I didn't want to see a psychiatrist, especially one with limited knowledge of trauma-based mind control and its effects. In my experience, higher levels of secular training equaled less dependence on the Lord. And that added up to more brain and less heart. I'd certainly had enough of living like that. No, only someone who heard clearly from God and who had a profound depth of faith would do. My prayerful yet desperate search continued.

And "she" turned out to be "he."

My introduction to John had been about four years earlier. He'd been the coordinator for an inner healing seminar I was attending, Ancient Paths II, which emphasized healing from shame. I'd been to the first level of Ancient Paths a year before as required by Family Foundations International, the presenting ministry and John's employer.

I don't remember all that much about meeting him, just that he'd prayed for me.

His memories of our first encounter aren't nearly so benign. He tells me I looked at him like he was Jack the Ripper. O-kaaay.

Anyway, part of John's job as the coordinator was to help the facilitators when they ran into trouble. These inner healing seminars attracted broken people—that was their purpose. And when you get that many wounds together in one room, the facilitators commonly struggle to minister effectively to at least one person.

Sheryl and Grayson were highly experienced facilitators, and they ministered with loving hearts. Everyone trusted them.

They just couldn't get through to me.

I sat hunched over in a folding chair, staring at the floor, away from the other participants. Sheryl and Grayson were trying to help me. I didn't realize how shut down and unable to respond I was because that was essentially my normal state. Eventually, they succumbed to my emotional inaccessibility and called in the coordinator for support.

John laid his hand on my shoulder (after asking my permission—I hadn't experienced much of that in my life) and prayed. I have no idea what he said, but some of my reserves collapsed. I fell into a puddle of tears. When I'd calmed down, he asked if he could give me a hug. I grabbed a tissue and told him to wait a minute. Sure didn't want to rub my drippy nose on his shirt!

I was frankly shocked that a stranger could have penetrated my defenses. Of course, it was God's love I'd felt, I just didn't know it. And years later John told me God had given him an unusual depth of love for me that day. That love was to become an unbreakable cord between us when he later became my new counselor.

The emerging connections didn't stop there. Sheryl and Grayson, as well as Paulette and David (who led the first seminar I'd attended at Family Foundations International) apparently saw something promising in me. A couple of years after initially encountering John, I was invited to become a volunteer small group facilitator for the same ministry: FFI.

John taught the weekend training program, making certain we understood one thing: "This training qualifies you to do absolutely nothing."

What?

Every one of us had to submit our agenda to God. We had to hear His voice and follow His direction. We should expect to struggle. The only failure would be if we ignored the Lord. And assistance would always be available.

I became a secondary facilitator working with small groups under John's continued supervision. He learned a lot about me, and I learned to trust him. That trust developed so rapidly because the Ancient Path lectures were on video, and as the participants watched and learned, the facilitators prayed for one another as well as for their groups. As for me, opening up became more comfortable as we all grew closer.

John's own prayer counseling ministry opened about the same time Phoebe was closing hers. Just as before, I had only a few weeks without a counselor's support. God orchestrated yet another alteration in my life, one that didn't require developing a new relationship.

We didn't have to tiptoe along while cautiously trying to get acquainted. No need to gradually establish a therapeutic connection.

No, John and I plunged right into my darkness.

STOICISM

The stoic lives in self-imposed stiffness.
Emotions are foreign
Except that of confusion
Because you are different
And that of contempt
Because you know you are to blame.
When anger or grief force their way into your
    consciousness
You are appalled
And wary
Because of their alien nature.
What to do with them?
Expression is out of the question
And you don't know how, anyway,
So they are buried;
Stuffed under a layer of intellectualism
And hidden within jokes or sarcasm.
But on rare occasions, they are no longer allowed
To be isolated
Because they are part of your destiny
And deserve to be known.
Then you reach out for help.
Professionals are safer
Because they don't know about
The real you.
Sometimes they are special.
A relationship grows—
One of compassion
And surprising trust.
Eventually

Vulnerability and exposure.
And you understand that though it is
a professional relationship,
it is yet a caring and
a helping relationship.
And through the confusion
And through the contempt,
Somehow, deep inside you know,
It will be all right.

5

Perceptions

⧈

Every session with John started with an update. Events from everyday life, a bit from my work, some material from odd dreams. You know: stuff.

Beyond that, little of our time was spent in conversation. God had to be the main communicator.

The very thought of the impending work overwhelmed me so many times. Why, *why* did I have to do this yet again?

Motivation fell apart. I stalled. Conversation meandered as I tried to postpone the inevitable.

John interrupted. "Well, we could just go for coffee, but that wouldn't help anything."

"Yeah, I know."

I was paying for this discomfort. I couldn't waste John's time and my money.

He was right. Again. "Ready to begin?"

I stared at him in silence.

Then he gave me a sympathetic little grin. "Ready as you'll ever be?"

A deep sigh and a nod signified my reluctant surrender.

I usually had to state out loud my willingness to submit to God's leading and to put a tight rein on my analytical tendencies. Easy? Not at all, especially early on. No, it went more like this:

"Lord Jesus, I give You permission to touch my feelings. Help me be willing to feel them as deeply as I need to. I choose to open my heart to You."

Just hearing this declaration made it more real to the "little ones" and to the present me. I said it reluctantly and without feeling any certainty or peace.

"Get out of your head!" It seemed John had to remind me during every session—and often more than once.

I sighed (or groaned) and reached for my water bottle, again disrupting the pattern of dependence on my own rational mind. "Okay. Just a minute."

And then I tried again, closing my eyes and eventually sinking into the hidden traumas that rose from my psyche. Memories drifted or even jumped into my consciousness—sometimes memories that had started leaking days or weeks before.

Memory leakage is a real phenomenon. Most counselors believe it's due to aging of the brain, since it usually starts to occur around age forty. My recent symptoms of post-traumatic stress disorder and vocal cord dysfunction were evidence of leakage.

Consider this: A dam that is consistently full will eventually develop tiny cracks and fissures. If it isn't reinforced or the pressure released, those fissures will become gushing fountains and the dam will crumble from the constant force of the water it's trying to hold back.

Our minds act in the same way. They try to hold back the hideous images, feelings, and fears, but sooner or later bits and pieces start to escape. The person wonders about their own mental stability; worries about what's happening to them; and, hopefully, seeks help. This is much too hard (possibly even dangerous) to deal with alone.

I remember struggling to describe the pictures playing across my mental screen—awful, terrifying, fragmented images of occult ceremonies. They never made any sort of sense. But I saw them. And I felt them.

This was a no-win situation. Fear crippled me: fear from the memories coupled with the fear that John would think I was making all this up. That I was just crazy.

My voice trembled. "I promise, I am not pretending. This is what I see."

John replied sadly, "No, I've heard other clients say something a lot like that. Way too often."

Early on, we discovered that the most common method of trauma-based mind control with this Masonic group was pure evil deception. A particularly strong memory:

A voice behind me said, "There's a snake crawling up your leg. Don't move an inch or it'll bite you. You'll die." I couldn't see a thing. I was too afraid to bend and look at the snake that I felt moving up my leg. Then, I felt a sharp sting and knew that mean old snake had stuck its fangs into my right hip. I blacked out.

I slowly regained consciousness as I heard the voice say, "You didn't listen to us. You are a bad girl. That snake bit you and you died. But we have the power to bring you back to life."

The adult me (who was listening to God's truth in John's office) realized that either I had been blindfolded or I'd closed my eyes in terror while one of the men drew something up my leg to simulate the feeling of a snake.

Fake snake but very real fear.

Then they injected me with a sedative. When I woke from the drugged sleep, I was groggy and unable to refute the lie that they had brought me back to life. The confused child believed the deception.

John commonly made this request: "Lord, please open her spiritual eyes." This rescued me from the deception many, many times as I saw the truth.

Another example of their devious torment: "Our leader is so powerful that he can stand in the middle of the fire and not get burned." My mind saw the man in the green robe surrounded by fire.[6] He was calm and even smiling. How could he not be afraid? Any sane person would have been! The hellish image inspired fear and awe. And it deepened my confusion.

Once again: "Lord, please open her spiritual eyes." The deception that little girl was unable to see came into focus as my vision widened. The man stood in the center of a circle of pipe. The fire came from a myriad of tiny gas jets. He was never in any danger as long as he minimized his movements.

One of the most prevalent arguments against utilizing repressed memories is that they are "inaccurate." To all appearances, they do seem inaccurate to the adult mind. But these memories are unearthed from within the child's mind, where they are stored virtually intact until brought into the conscious mind. Any parent (or older relative or childcare worker) can tell you that childish perceptions are very different from adult perceptions.

Even a group of adults can perceive the same incident differently from one another. Imagine a horrific motor vehicle accident on a busy street corner. Some adults will remember the actual collision: how the car rose up at impact, how it sounded when it hit the streetlamp, how it smelled when the fuel spilled out. They will not have perceived the passengers' screams.

Other people will perceive only the people crying for help and remember feeling frozen in place. Still others will perceive (as if in slow motion) bystanders rushing to render aid but will recall little about the collision itself.

If perception is that varied within a group of adults, doesn't it make sense that a child's traumatic memories will reflect the child's perspective? And that perspective will be affected by fear and confusion? Everything looks huge to a small child. An object that the adult sees as innocuous will cause terror in the child.

Why? Filters and experience. A child has not developed the informational and emotional filters utilized by adults. These come through maturity and life experience.

Another common argument says that repressed memories are planted by therapists. A secular therapist might be able to implant a memory into a suggestible client through repetition and manipulation. Of course, this action would put them on the same base level as the cults who manipulate children—an illegal and completely unethical activity. An ethical, caring therapist would never think about doing that, either in a secular or a faith-based practice.

I don't believe an adult survivor who is going through all this will receive the infrequent suggestion. I know I couldn't. On the rare occasion John did offer an idea, he did it with the clear understanding that it was mine to test for inner validity and then to take or leave. And I knew if

John's words didn't ring as completely accurate and true to me, they were to be rejected. No problem.

Often his words helped me clarify my own expressions of what I was feeling, but John never tried to force his opinion on me. Frankly, I wouldn't have accepted it. It would have been like an ill-fitting shoe—uncomfortable at best, damaging at worst.

We were working on a deeply spiritual level, allowing God to speak to our hearts and minds. He was the only One who could speak truth to my heart. And I knew He wouldn't lie or manipulate me.

I did discover a few memories that had been planted by the cult, as well as one or two that my own mind had substituted for the real ones. In every instance, the implanted or substituted memory was discovered to be a milder version of the real one. It was done to hide the agonizing truth, either to protect the cult or to protect my own mind and heart.

Which brings us to the third argument against the use of repressed memories: the child makes it all up to get attention. I want to scream, "Why would they?" Why would a child make up something so hideous they can't bear to look at it?

These memories are so horrendous the conscious mind can't handle it, so it turns away, allowing another part to deal with the pain. Those parts guard the memory, hold the pain, and protect the core person from further trauma.

So the memories stay hidden, walled off until the pressure builds enough to allow leaking. Then the person is more mature and may be ready to face the truth, strong enough to stand up to it, and more willing to work with the Healer for her ultimate recovery. It isn't easy, but it is necessary.

Like many of us from that era, I was told as a child, "Only cry when it's important." But what was important?

Who decided? It wasn't long before I simply didn't cry about anything. My internal judge was merciless with any weakness. I also feared that John would judge me harshly for this "flaw" until, from time to time, I heard him sniffle when I sat watching the mental videos and trying to tell him what I saw. *Is he crying?* I thought, *For me?*

It could have been allergies, but I chose to believe it was empathy that moved John to tears. His actions touched my heart, softening it with love and strengthening my resolve to get through the memories and the awful pain and confusion they caused.

John continually entered my darkness with me.

A few months after we started working together, I collided with the old roadblock of shutdown. Emotional overload froze me into inaccessibility. Nothing would release my pent-up emotion except tears or maybe fighting, but I literally couldn't cry and I certainly wouldn't hit anyone. I crossed my arms and held tight, a huddled, miserable girl hugging myself without comfort as I rocked back and forth. With eyes closed and jaw clenched, I couldn't see past the dark obstruction. Isolation deepened. Silence lengthened.

Then I heard John shift in his seat. "I feel like the Lord wants me to ask you something unusual. Would it be okay if I came over and gave you a hug?"

I nodded, the motion brittle, but no way could I open my arms or my eyes to welcome an expression of comfort.

He knelt on the floor in front of my chair and put his arms around my shoulders. One hand gently guided my head to his shoulder. I broke. Deep, shuddering sobs shook my body and choked my breathing. I wrapped my fingers in his sleeve and gripped it for dear life.

I don't ever remember weeping that hard or that long, not with someone there to comfort me—only when I was alone in the dark and berating myself unmercifully for being ugly or worthless or unlovable.

I'd learned in the FFI ministry facilitator training that we shouldn't comfort participants who were struggling. Other group members were also not allowed to touch them, no matter the personal relationship. It would be a distraction, interrupting the process and moving their focus from God to us.

Master's-level counseling classes agreed with the "distraction" premise, adding that it was unethical to allow a client to get that emotionally close. Unhealthy dependence (enmeshment) could result. Lawsuits could follow when the inevitable problems arose.

But this was different. This was intense, ongoing ministry. This was a demonstration of God's love, and completely necessary for me to learn that not all touch was defiling or painful. All men weren't to be feared. Some allowed God's hands to work through them when His touch was needed.

John called himself a "labor coach." He likened his efforts to when his wife gave birth. "She did the work; I just encouraged her and helped her focus. That's what we're doing here. We're a team—you, me, and God.

"And we will get through this."

So, I went through the labor of the memories, lies, and pain, and John coached me while God healed.

WHAT DO I WANT?

I want to know who I am, not who I am expected to be
- to feel comfortable in my own skin, not like an alien in disguise
- to be happy, not just act like it
- to be fulfilled, not fill a role
- to be loved, not tolerated
- to accept my feelings, not deny my right to them
- to be able to really relax, not to be always tense and defensive
- to be complete, not divided
- to have hope, not despair
- to have peace, not numbness
- to have self-love, not self-pity
- to be able to trust, not constantly fear
- to be able to love without suspicion
- to be able to be wrong without feeling diminished
- to be able to be right without feeling defensive
- to be confident in who I am, not just in what I can do
- to have a home, not just a hiding place
- to have friends, not just acquaintances
- to feel like a woman, not just a person
- to have a husband who loves God and me, not just a dream of romance
- to have a quiet mind, like David, not a tormented one, like Saul
- to be healed completely, not wondering if it is possible
- to be released, not bound to the past
- to be me, the "me" I was meant to be
- to be a butterfly, not a caterpillar
- to be attractive and active, seeking and enjoying life

    courageous and unafraid
    open and honest . . .
    . . . FREE . . .

Is that too much to ask?

6

The Truth Will Set You Free

Mid-2002

John tells me he wondered how I could trust him so much when we started working together. Why hadn't I sought out another female counselor?

When I was just beginning my healing journey with Phoebe, I also had quite an experience with John. At the time I only knew him from the Ancient Paths II conference when he'd ministered to me, but he's the one who introduced me to the practice of Theophostic Prayer Ministry (TPM). It's not counseling per se but a system of ministry and was the first technique that offered real help to me. I'd seen psychotherapists in the past for depression and stress management but talk therapy had done nothing. Antidepressants had produced no relief. Even my own praying hadn't helped much because my true issues were so deeply hidden.

Ed Smith, founder of TPM, coined the title from two Greek terms: *Theo*, meaning "God," and *phós* meaning "light." (The title has since been changed to "Transformation Prayer Ministry.")

Phoebe had told me she thought I would do well with TPM but wanted me to learn about it beforehand to be certain I understood and accepted the process. She broached the subject late in our third session. "I think you'd do nicely if we utilized Theophostic. People with dissociation are a great fit for TPM, and I've seen quite a bit of success with it. I have a book you should read so we can discuss it ahead of time and you can decide for yourself."

Phoebe rummaged through her crowded bookcase until she realized her error. "Oh, that's right! Sorry. I loaned it to someone else and it's still out. Guess I'll have to give them a call. I doubt I can get it to you before I leave on my trip, though."

We hesitated to start a complex conversation in our limited amount of remaining session time, so she gave a simple outline of the procedure: "This is how it works: Basically, we follow your pain along the path God takes us and then He reveals the memory that's causing the lie you believe. That's where the pain comes from. Then we invite Jesus into the memory and He will bring truth to counter the lie. That heals the pain."

I was left wondering about what she'd said and hoping the book would find its way home soon. Since I'm more of a visual learner, Phoebe's verbal explanation hadn't quite done the job. And she left town just a few days later.

I was still terrified about the vocal cord dysfunction and what it might mean, not to mention being afraid it would get worse. My voice hadn't improved. A vital part of my job, it was still iffy and had a bad habit of giving out at the most inconvenient times. Any coughing or minor choking episodes could set off an attack. Sometimes it tightened up when I simply turned my head. I couldn't sing at all, either, and I greatly missed my thirty-plus years of participating in church choir.

My Personal Holocaust

No matter how hard I searched within, I couldn't unearth any reassurances. Would my fear ever leave? Would it even improve? Would I ever be normal? Phoebe and I hadn't worked together long enough—I knew we had barely begun. That may have been the worst stage in the journey: knowing help was available but realizing neither of us had any idea how long it would take or how much work would be needed. I was unbelievably tired of the uncertainty, but fighting the fear was what really drained me.

Phoebe had been out of town for a couple of weeks, but I had to talk to somebody right away! Who else might know me well enough? Whom could I trust with this weirdness? Grayson and Sheryl came to my mind. Maybe my old FFI mentors could help. I called their number and tried to explain my situation and ask them to pray for me. I simply couldn't live with this paralyzing fear much longer!

"You know, I think you should talk to John about this," Sheryl advised. "I believe he's out of town right now, but leave him a message. We'll be praying for you." She provided his phone number.

Slightly confused and still very much afraid, I left a message for John on Wednesday evening. The following Sunday afternoon, he returned my call.

"Sorry about the wait. I was on a camping trip with my son." Then he said something odd. "My wife and I have prayed about this, and we don't feel like we should become your counselors."

What? I had a perfectly good counselor! I'd finally be seeing her at Bible study that evening . . . why was all this so hard? All I needed was prayer for the fear! I told him as much, trying to express myself clearly without sounding obnoxious.

"Oh." I could practically hear John nod. "Of course I'll pray for you." He paused. "But maybe we could try something right now. Would that be okay?"

At this point, I would agree to practically anything that had to do with prayer from someone I trusted, however embryonic that trust was. I desperately needed to get a decent night's sleep. Anxiety was pushing my blood pressure through the roof. Decision-making took more effort than ever.

After some hesitation and a deep breath, I replied, "Okay."

I sat cross-legged on the kitchen floor and closed my eyes. John proceeded to lead me—over the phone—through an old memory of a frightening dream from when I was eight or nine years old. I saw myself in the dream: I was in a field, and a wildfire overtook me until I was surrounded by flames, with no help in sight. Barely breathing, trembling, terrified right there in the kitchen . . . from an obscure memory!

Just as Phoebe had described to me a couple weeks before, God had reminded me of the dream and then John and I followed the fear to its source: my feelings of being lost, alone, and helpless. Of being afraid I was going to die a painful death. We invited Jesus to come into the dream and bring truth. In my mind's eye I saw Him pick me up and knew we were safe even from the raging prairie fire. The fire was still there, but I was safe and no longer alone.

About forty minutes passed. When my emotional storm subsided, John asked if I felt more peace.

I agreed . . . kind of. The fear unearthed by the dream was gone, but, "Well, I don't really feel anything."

"Sounds like that could be peace." John's voice held a combination of humor and calm. The effect deepened my trust in him.

A few hours later, I met Phoebe at our weekly Bible study and told her about what I'd experienced that afternoon. Then, following a hunch, I asked, "Is that Theophostic?"

"That's it."

We agreed to proceed. If something so simple could be so effective on my terror, sign me up!

I never did get to read the book until I took the courses myself. Didn't matter, anyway. Our work proceeded just fine until the day Phoebe closed her practice in September 2001.

November 2001

John, like Phoebe, had also completed the apprenticeship-level training and had had success in working with ritual abuse survivors. When we began our association, it meant I joined the small group of traumatized and dissociative women in his client list. Not exactly a highly desired membership, but a valuable one. Only a few local counselors and ministers were trained in and utilizing advanced TPM at that time. Other highly effective prayer and healing techniques were available, but most were several years from being quantified and widely practiced.

Not very many counselors were willing to put forth the effort that would be required; this wouldn't be a one- or two-year therapeutic relationship. Nothing would be straightforward. Not that many were willing to allow God to love these difficult clients through them—to feel and communicate His unconditional love for as long as it took. If you ask John about working with survivors, he'll say it's a calling. "If you aren't called to the work, don't even try to do it. It's just too hard. And you have to depend on God's grace to get through it."

There was no way to predict, even loosely, how long the healing journey would take. John simply refused to even hazard a guess. I believe his comment was something like "Only God knows." We had no choice but to move forward with no end in sight.

I remember sending him lots of discouraged emails asking, "Is this ever going to be over?"

"Yes, it will," he replied. "Be patient with yourself. Be strong. God is working, and I won't give up on you. And when we are through it, I hope we can still be good friends."

John taught me early on that my healing was dependent on my choices. Sometimes having to choose really got my anger up.

He often asked, "Is it all right if we go to that memory?" (or that place, or whatever).

I replied, "I don't want to go there. It's too scary." (This was usually the child speaking. I was listening in.)

"That's okay. It's up to you. It's completely your choice."

Just when I wanted sympathy, John made me choose what to do! Fortunately, my anger always morphed into more of a challenge. You know—the old "You think I'm chicken, don't you? Well, I'll show you!"

As if that weren't frustrating enough, John had this other question up his sleeve: "It's okay if you don't go there, but what would happen if you did?" or, alternately, "if you didn't?" That led to another choice. Would I let Jesus take care of business as He always did, or would I rebel and call a halt to my progress, at least for that day?

And progress we did, through unbelievable pain, unfathomable fear, and unrelenting doubt; through anger, rage, shame—defining the feelings wasn't always important as long as we followed them to the memories and the lies.

We asked Jesus for His truth in all those dark places, and He gradually brought His light into my emotional and mental darkness. Most important, He never allowed me to be completely overwhelmed by the pain.

RIPTIDE

The ocean . . .
    Compelling, powerful,
    Life-filled and mysterious.
To swim here evokes peace
    and caution.
As I swim in Life's ocean
    I am cautious . . .
    Unknown dangers lurk
       amidst the beauty.
Floating along, rocked by gentle waves,
    Enjoying peace . . . until
RIPTIDE!
    No fight will conquer it.
       It saps my will and strength—
       Confuses my mind,
       Changes my direction.
My life plays out before me
    (as, is said, happens before dying)
and, though not what I would have chosen,
    It is yet mine, and
    Not easily surrendered.
But riptide carries me where I would not go
    And laughs at my struggle.
I am afraid.
    Exhaustion consumes me . . .
    Muscles weaken,
    Breath tightens.
I have one choice—
    Surrender or fight.
    One is certain death,
    The other less certain.

My Personal Holocaust

Are my struggles all for nothing?
    Time shortens, Light dims . . .
I am afraid . . .
    Not of the dying,
    But of the failure.

7

False versus True Memories

"These memories can't be real! Who would do such awful things to a little kid?"

John reassured me of their validity. He sadly told me of hearing very similar things from other clients. Other ritual abuse survivors.

My emotions vacillated between rage, confusion, and grief. The more sessions I had with John, the more scenes of abuse God revealed to me and the more I asked myself if any of this could be real. Could I be making them up?

Finally, desperation shaded my queries. I asked John for clarification.

"The average mind can't wrap around that kind of evil because it hasn't submitted itself to it. People's minds simply can't go there. But when the evil begins to take over, those people can't help but go there, and even further.

"It's like we read in Jeremiah 7: 'Walk in all the ways that I have commanded you, so that it may be well with you. But they did not listen nor bow their ear. But *they walked in their own plans, in the stubbornness of their evil heart, and went backward and not forward*' [LITV, emphasis added].

"And the reverse is also true. Once we submit our minds to God and continue in that path, we get further and further from evil imaginings. Eventually we can't even make our minds engage in evil thoughts."

At last, something that made sense. When John used that context, I could accept that my memories were real. I couldn't be making them up. My redeemed, conscious mind simply wouldn't go there. And no way could I be innocently conjuring up that level of pain.

Then other questions arose. What if false memories showed up in my mind during a ministry session? Would I be able to recognize them as false? Would I just accept them as being true, not knowing the difference?

So it boils down to this important question: Are "false memories" really false?

Imagine this scene: Two adult sisters are talking about something that happened when they were four and eight years old.

"I'm telling you, he molested me! Our father put his hands on me and touched me between my legs. Whenever I think about it, I feel so dirty!" The younger sister lowers her head in her hands, sobbing in shame and anger.

"That never happened, not like you mean! I was there," the older one declares. "I know. Trust me." She lays a hand on her kid sister's arm, but the comforting gesture causes more angry weeping and pulling away.

Question: Is the memory true or false?

Answer: Yes.

Each memory is true as far as the sisters know. But each has false—actually, incomplete—segments.

The younger remembers the touch, remembers it was her father, but doesn't remember why it happened. She does remember being frightened and in pain.

False versus True Memories

The older also remembers their father touching the little girl and does remember why it happened. She remembers being worried about her sister. And about her own fear of getting in trouble because she was supposed to be watching out for her.

The truth is that the younger sister fell off her first two-wheel bike, landing astraddle the bar. It hurt, to say the least. And her father examined her inside their house a little while later to determine if the damage might require a trip to the emergency room. Mom wasn't available at the time, so he couldn't call on her. His fear for the daughter's safety also affected the wounded little girl, and when the memory surfaced, she misinterpreted that fear as being his guilt.

There really is no such thing as a completely false memory. Something happened, and the mind stored it virtually intact while hiding it from the core person. The falseness arises with misinterpretation. And with repeated telling, the memory tends to become more distorted.

Returning to the scenario: the older sister explains to the younger exactly what happened, how she was hurt and how both the sister and the father were worried about her. The explanation is a little hard for the younger girl to believe at first, but knowing what kind of man their father is enables her to realize that the reality is consistent with his character and with his customary treatment of his beloved daughters.

Her devastating internal pain had arisen because of the dichotomy in her mind and emotions. She faced a terrible inner struggle: "How could a man I love and have always known to be honorable hurt me like that? Can I still love him or do I have to hate him? I can't do both at the same time!" This mental contradiction and its attending emotional struggle is a setup for dissociation.

It's an irresolvable conflict.

Now imagine the younger sister has kept her secret from her immediate family members while seeing a therapist who encourages her to confront the father and take him to court in the name of "emotional resolution." The thought makes me cringe. No inner healing exists there. This action tears apart not only families but the individuals in those families.

The therapist, as a trusted confidant and neutral party, should indeed believe the story but should also seek the truth, knowing the story is a child's perception. And if it's an old enough memory, the truth may be humanly impossible to find because the participants may be dead or otherwise unavailable. Bringing legal action doesn't provide emotional resolution; it often makes things worse. Only God can reveal the truth and heal the pain. And after all, isn't the ultimate goal healing rather than vengeance?

Do I remember finding false (better term: falsified) memories? I do, but only a few. After the first one appeared, I was able to tell they were false by two things. First, they tended to be in black and white instead of in color when projected on my mental viewing screen. And there was a niggling feeling in the back of my mind—a kind of warning: "Hey, heads up! Something's wrong here."

The first memory I remember being false was when I saw myself in a tall, narrow, dark building (kind of like a two-story outhouse without the privy) and black birds were flying above my head. I was locked in with no way of escape as the birds dive-bombed me periodically. I narrated the picture to John as it played, even while feeling off. My fear and pain didn't seem intense enough, not as it was in the other memories.

Later I realized that I had seen it in black and white and that God was sending me the off feeling to reveal the truth.

This memory was either implanted by the cult to cover up something they had done, or it was something I had made up to protect myself from the authentic emotional or physical trauma. Either way, it was clearly not false, but incomplete. We couldn't process it; Jesus wouldn't enter the memory because it hadn't actually happened in the presenting form.

However, we could, and did, ask Him to heal the pain and confusion.

This memory taught me how to distinguish falsified from factual. When another falsified memory emerged, I could reject it with the clarity given by God. There weren't many of them. I truly could count them on my fingers. Most of my revealed memories were indeed true, even if distorted a bit from being seen by the child.

When a memory proved to be falsified, Jesus was faithful to show me the truth after we asked Him to do it. That truth was usually much worse than the false memory, but He was there to reassure me of His love, and to heal and restore. Jesus freely entered the factual, historical portion of the memory.

This all boils down to one thing: there is no such thing as a false memory. Distorted, overlaid, falsified by the self or the cult, yes, but not completely false. Something happened and the child took it to be true. She had no choice at the time. No filters.

And it doesn't matter whether the memory leaned more toward false or toward true. What is important is what lie the child believed about it and herself, and how that lie affected her. That effect is what God heals with His truth and love.

But God usually doesn't heal someone without a team effort. Someone has to be the coach, has to keep track of the details. This entire process is too complicated to handle alone.

Another very important factor in recovery is the relationship between the survivor and the counselor. If I hadn't deeply trusted that John listened to God's wisdom above his own, I probably would have had neither the confidence nor the ability to discard questions or suggestions that rang potentially false in my heart. Because I trusted John, I was also able to trust myself and what I felt God was saying to me.

I could finally trust my own heart.

I have known other survivors who have not received the same level of healing as I. I've often wondered about that. Had they struggled for years while searching for answers—and generally in the wrong places?

We know that highly intelligent and highly educated people tend to be analytical—they like to solve complex issues and they enjoy fixing things. But putting knowledge into a person's mind is not the answer. I cannot emphasize this enough: intellectual learning can't heal. Believe me: I've tried.

The worst result from all this "forever learning and never able to come to a knowledge of the truth" (2 Timothy 3:7, paraphrased) is that the survivor more willingly believes that anything that God shows them is actually something they read or heard about from someone else.

Wounded counselors tend to struggle with this more than other survivors. My heart aches for those caught in this trap. It's something I managed to avoid, whether by my own good judgment or from God's guidance (most likely from both). I refused to do any research or compare notes with other survivors until after I had been in counseling for several years.

False versus True Memories

My best guess is that I reached out during my sixth year. That was when I attended a "Freedom from Freemasonry" weekend seminar presented by Joe and Sara King, who had come from England to minister. By then I had learned quite well to avoid trying to do the work on my own, within my own mind. But I didn't do a lot more studying beyond that seminar until much later.

We logic-focused people tend to have a terrible time putting our brains on the back burner and surrendering our thoughts to the One who made us. I struggled intensely with this. I had to learn how to trust beyond my ability to reason. It was tough since I'd been depending on my mind to protect and defend me up until that time. Practice and persistence had to prevail. But, as with any effort, the more I worked at it, the easier it became and the less frequently John had to remind me.

However, eventually my analytical tendencies tripped me up. That was the time—which comes to us all—when I had just about convinced myself that it was all made-up. All from my own imagination. Picked up from somewhere, even if I couldn't remember it clearly.

My sessions with John were always a safe place to be. Even when I felt threatened while going through traumatic memories, somehow I knew God was protecting me from destruction and John was supporting our efforts.

This day I brought my fearful doubt to the forefront. John and I discussed it.

"None of this is real, right? It couldn't have happened. It's just nuts! Why would these people even do this to me?" Was I in denial or something?

John had always believed me when I narrated even the most bizarre memories. But could I believe me anymore?

My Personal Holocaust

The only thing I absolutely knew to be real was the deep, gut-wrenching emotional pain. Real pain. Real confusion. Real despair. This couldn't have all have come from my imagination! I wasn't crazy—first Phoebe and then John had reaffirmed it. Repeatedly.

I'd watched scary movies when I was younger; none of the pretend mayhem bothered me all that much. Frightening made-up scenes certainly didn't emerge as repressed memories when I was an adult. I needed the truth. I had to ask the only One who had been there with me through it all. No way around it.

Courage was always easier to find when I felt safe. And the safest place was always John's office. Deep breath. "God, if this is real, I want to know. Prove it. Show me." And then I waited.

The mental movie started. Figures formed. Four men stood around me, glowering. One held my portrait—the only one my folks had had professionally done. I was an adorable one-year-old. The leader angrily jabbed his finger at the framed eight-by-ten-inch photograph. "This isn't you! You are who we say you are!"

My heart sank. My stomach twisted. I knew. All this—the images, the repressed memories, the torment—was real.

It mattered not one iota that this portrait was well-known to me, and they might not have actually held it. I knew. Deep inside, I knew.

My pain, my confusion, my despair, my dissociation—all were real. All had a cause. And that cause was trauma-based mind control. Ritual abuse. Purposeful, deliberate torment of a child.

Me.

Bile threatened to rise; for a moment I fought to keep my breakfast.

John said, "I need a bathroom break. Be right back." He closed the office door as he quietly exited, leaving me briefly alone to ponder what I had seen and to let it settle in.

And to ask God what to do next.

I stared dully at the floor for a few moments and then stepped to the window. Surely a bit of sunshine would offer some relief. It didn't. I gripped the frame and rested my head on my forearm. Deeply buried tears couldn't come near my eyes. Why did the rock in my chest keep beating when I knew it must be dead?

John came back in, shut the door behind him, and walked over to me. I heard him. I didn't move. Didn't open my eyes.

He laid a hand on my shoulder. "You okay?"

I pulled away.

"Not okay, huh?"

I shook my head. Returned to the couch. Sat down. Felt like I'd taken a gut punch. Why had I ever asked for proof?

But God had honored my desperate request and my true situation. He had sent me proof that I could accept. I never asked again.

For several years, whenever I leaned toward disbelief, I could pull out that memory and look at it. And I knew it was real.

I never needed any more proof.

8

The Science of Memory

The brain is a mysterious place. The process of memory has long been—and in many ways remains—an enigma.

By now you might be in the group of readers thinking, *How can this be real? How could anyone have abuse like this happen and not remember it?* And, of course, *How could childhood memories be authentic after all this time?* I've wondered about all that. I've also gone through the "daylighting" of repressed traumatic memories. Experience is a powerful teacher.

Let's talk about repressed memories. I'm sure you've seen something like this:

> The toddler plunked himself down onto the concrete floor. He had earlier gazed in fascination at the sparkling display of shiny faucets, but no more. Tired and hungry, he wanted his daddy. But daddy was not in view. Now fear joined the emotional ranks.
>
> "Daddy! Daddy!" The still air in the home improvement warehouse carried his terrified little voice to his father's ears at the far end of the aisle.

The Science of Memory

Two people appeared in only a moment: his father and the store employee he'd been speaking with as he walked away from the boy. The crying child reached chubby arms up to his daddy. After a few more shuddering sobs, he calmed in his daddy's arms.

"I got you, son. It's okay."

The employee smiled tightly. "Sure he's all right, sir?"

"Oh, yeah. He won't remember any of this. He's too little."

The memory is repressed in the child's mind. It may surface later or remain there for his lifetime, but it never disappears. He does remember; the electrochemical processes of the brain ensure it. Even unintended occurrences with no ill intentions, such as a tipped stroller, will be stored if they are sufficiently traumatic to the individual child.

Anybody who still believes that small children don't remember traumatic events, raise your hand and repeat after me, "That's just propaganda."

What if the cults have had a hand in perpetuating this lie to gloss over their actions? Or did they just take advantage of "common knowledge"?

This arena of common knowledge has lost much of its validity recently. Although spiritual truths and approaches to emotional healing have been pooh-poohed in the past, medical science and technology have been quietly catching up in recent years. Brain science (neurobiology) has been advancing rapidly.

As recently as the 1980s, scientists assumed the adult brain was unchangeable. However, newer brain scans (MRI, PET, and SPECT) have revealed the truth. Although brain activity slows with age, it never stops. Through the function of neuroplasticity, the brain can produce new cells and modify existing ones. New connections are created between cells throughout its lifespan as the brain continually rewires itself, adapting to life changes.

The scientific community also assumed young children's ability to remember was minimal or nonexistent. The true issue is that even after youngsters learn to speak, they don't yet have the vocabulary to describe what happened, so they can't share the memory with anyone else. How many parents have listened to what seemed like nonsensical babbling as their small child told them what had happened on the playground? I remember my father once telling me I didn't have a brain in my head when I tried to describe, in my child words, my concern that our outdoor faucet had an ice dam and might cause a flood. Of course, my description was inadequate, and he lost patience.

The assumption that children aren't supposed to be able to recall events any earlier than the age of four or five years (and certainly without accurate detail) is just that: an assumption.

My own life has knocked that theory sideways. I remember falling down the stairs and into the basement of my parents' new home when I was barely three. Driving in the family station wagon to my grandfather's house one night through a fierce blizzard. Tripping and landing in a puddle at an amusement park kiddie ride after the rain stopped. And being given a pink polio vaccine on a sugar cube. All of these are conscious memories.

All before I turned five.

The Science of Memory

We know that children perceive time differently from grown-ups. Witness the traditional, "Are we there yet?" query as an impatient child travels to some desired but apparently distant destination. (Of course, if you ask the adult about it, the toy store is only fifteen minutes away!)

Torture lasting a few minutes for a child seems interminable to her, while torture lasting several hours or days for an adult may not break the soldier. And lest we forget, a childhood memory does not resemble an adult one because of the experience and filters that are developed with maturity.

When children are traumatized, the brain stores the memory until the truth is revealed years later, whether through flashbacks, secular therapeutic intervention, or ministry.

This same process of mental storage and recovery occurs with adult traumatic memories. I was still a PA student when I was assigned to the locked psych ward at the Veterans Administration Hospital (VA). It seemed a benign place for the first week or two. I made friends with the medical staff and performed my patient care tasks. A depressed patient even taught me how to play pool.

But one morning, as I approached the door, keys at the ready, I heard shouting. Once inside the hallway, I saw the source. An older veteran crouched against the wall, terrified and trembling, covering his head with his hands.

"Incoming! Incoming!" His screams permeated the normally quiet ward. I'd never seen manifestations of PTSD and didn't know what I should do except report to the staff. Frankly, I was a little scared.

What I was seeing was an *abreaction*. Hawkins defines it as "the recall of a traumatic memory in its original, unprocessed, sensory and affective form in which the vivid re-experience of sight, sound, touch, taste, smell, and emotions make it seem like a re-living of the event."[7]

Not all abreactions are this intense. In general, the more extreme the original trauma, the stronger the abreaction. A memory that has been partially processed will commonly initiate milder responses as healing progresses.

Oh, I had some doozies. Though the adult me almost always felt safe in John's office, the process of memory work exhausted me early on and I had to take a two-hour nap when I got home. I know my fatigue was not simply physical but also from emotional strain.

The session notes don't reflect much detail about abreactions, but I remember them. Often, curiosity reigned as I watched a scene start to unfold in my mind. That curiosity quickly devolved into fear as I (in the child mind) wondered what those bad men would do next. I fearfully questioned why they were tormenting me and promised to be good if only they would let me go home. How could I make them stop?

My body twitched as feelings of electric shock or other painful physical and emotional sensations surfaced. In the present, I couldn't control my physical reactions. If I tried, they got worse.

Pain appeared in various parts of my body. I regularly felt a left/right split. Sometimes it felt as though one side was shrinking while the other remained the same.

I wept desperate, uncontrollable tears as I watched events unfold. Sometimes the terror was so great I almost forced my way through the back of the sofa I was sitting on. When I could no longer describe the scene in words, I drew pictures with a child's technique. With crayons, no less.

Through it all, John's voice was my lifeline. He continually asked God to strengthen me and to only let me see what was important for healing. John reassured the terrified youngster and helped her understand that we were not physically in that place anymore.

June 2003

JOHN: So, what are you sensing?

ADULT PERSONA: *Not much. The only thing I'm sensing is a division, right down the middle. The right side feels smaller than the left. Almost like it's actively shrinking at this point.*

It feels like there's a fear of disappearing. Of everybody on the right side going into the left side. This makes no sense at all! And it feels like muscle tension on the right but the left side is relaxed.

More images float by.

JOHN: What are you feeling now?

I jump at hearing the question, startled.

LITTLE ONE: *I want to go to sleep [dissociate] but they won't let me.*

JOHN: Lord, increase Your anointing and power. Show her what she needs to see there.

ADULT PERSONA: *My left hand is tingling, not my right, just the left. Like it's waking up from being asleep.*

I struggle to pull away from that painful sensation.

ADULT PERSONA: *I keep getting a picture of electrodes on all five fingers on my left hand. The left side of my body is twitching, but not the right. They tell me, "One side is good and one side is bad." It doesn't make sense!*

While I'm narrating the scenes, I am dizzy enough to sway and wobble . . . dizziness often precedes dissociation. Pain spreads through my head.

None of it ever makes sense.

Early in my healing journey, I attended a seminar on memory as part of my ministry training. The instructors discussed the hippocampus and the amygdala as parts of the brain involved in memory generation and processing.

It seems that "Amy" and "Hippo" are employed by the Brain Company, having offices adjacent to each other in the memory division.

Amy functions rather like an executive assistant. She receives incoming information at an incredibly rapid rate, and disseminates it electronically to the appropriate departments.

The more mundane and routine material lands in Hippo's inbox. His main job is to sort new data and correlate it with past experiences, making a coherent life record. This gets filed in a downloadable mental PDF that we (the CEO) can locate for recall. But Hippo doesn't stop there; he also designs links to connect our emotions and memories.

However, when Amy detects traumatic experiences, she sends them to a completely different floor, wherein resides a newly promoted, previously ignored employee,

The Science of Memory

PCC (posterior cingulate cortex). When anyone is granted access to his office, they quickly exit due to the chaos they often encounter there.

If the incoming data from a traumatic experience is too much for our sweet Amy, it overwhelms her. She swoons into a dead faint and the memory is blocked without being processed. When she comes to and is ready to get back to work, she doesn't remember what happened.

What? You didn't know we have a soap opera constantly playing in our minds?

All right, then. Time to return to real life.

So, the hippocampus remains somewhat of a mystery, even though it has been studied extensively. It acts as a nursery of sorts,[8] creating new neurons and storing them for a short time. It also helps us incorporate a sense of ourselves related to space and time. Structurally, it's located near the center of the brain.

The amygdala is actually two halves of the same structure, with each half located at the sides of the brain near the hippocampus. It's been found to create the feelings we associate with fear and trauma.

Neither region actively stores memories of any kind. However, decades of research with military veterans and survivors of sexual assault have revealed that traumatic memories somehow function differently from other memories.[9]

Seeking experimental evidence for this premise, a group of researchers from Yale University and from Icahn School of Medicine (New York) studied a group of posttraumatic stress disorder (PTSD) sufferers. These subjects listened to self-recorded narrations from their own memories while undergoing brain scans. Some recorded memories were traumatic while others were neutral or involved some type of emotional upset, such as a death in the family.

Real-time images revealed distinct differences between the brain's responses to traumatic memories and more benign types. The hippocampus surprisingly did not respond when the subject listened to a traumatic memory narration. It appeared as though the scanned brain was not remembering anything stimulated by the narration but instead was experiencing something in the present.

The traumatic memories engaged an entirely different and unexpected area of the brain, the posterior cingulate cortex. The PCC has not historically been known as a memory region of the brain, but one that is involved with processing mental rather than physical experiences. It is generally involved in internal thought, such as daydreaming or meditation. But in this investigation, the more intense the PTSD responses were, the more activity was detected within the PCC.

The researchers concluded that traumatic memories are not experienced in the same manner as other memories but more as potent fragments of prior events. They overpower the present moment, not allowing other memories to interfere. This agrees with my own experiences.

During memory work sessions, I only saw/relived pieces of the torment. There was no way for me to reconstruct a complete storyline as I could when thinking about benign, conscious memories. My focus was usually on a single agonizing event. That event was sometimes revisited in later sessions, often from another perspective. Only God knew where we were going and what needed to be healed. Only He could arrange some sense out of all that craziness.

The Science of Memory

Cults are organized. They perform established ceremonies. They follow proven rituals handed down through the ages. They successfully deceive children and cause dissociation, even trying to program them with varying degrees of success.

Examples of ceremonies and torment are scattered throughout this book, but something few people think or talk about is preparing the child to "forget" before the ceremonies. This may also be an attempt to keep the child calm so she doesn't fight.

A commonly used tactic is called "sandwiching." A trusted adult takes the child to play in the park for a short while. Then they go to the lodge where the torment occurs. After it's over, the child is given something special, perhaps ice cream. From beginning to end, the entire episode lasts for only a brief time, likely less than an hour.

Tormenting a child into dissociation can be successful even when each repeated episode lasts only a few minutes. And the child will be unlikely to remember the torment; it's probable she'll only remember the pleasure of her sweet treat.

Similarly, marketers have successfully used this premise because adults also tend to remember the last thing they see or hear. Commercials will repeat phone numbers several times at the end of the ad, saying "Don't forget, call this number to learn about . . ."

And adults have filters and logic. The child has neither.

The repressed traumatic memories and the torment that caused them all add up to a heartbreaking tragedy: a stolen childhood.

IT ALL HURTS

My eyes hurt. I'm so tired of all this. There is a great emptiness inside,
and I can't cry anymore—it hurts too much
My head hurts. Anger and fear and sadness fight each other for dominance and I want it to go away
or I want to go away
There is no peace or happiness or joy to bubble to the surface—no surprise relief from the pain
And my head hurts and my heart hurts and I want it to stop.
Somehow, I thought it could never be as bad as before, when the pain had no identity—when it only hurt all the time and a cloud covered everything.
I was wrong.
I don't remember being so lost. I don't remember being so empty.
When people die, the loss is bad, but at least you have some happy memories to sustain you until the pain diminishes.
But I have lost too much, and happy memories don't exist. They never were. They just never were.
I am so tired of hearing "life isn't fair."
I am so tired of sucking it up.
I don't have the strength anymore.
I want God to prove to me that all this pain isn't capricious. It has to be more than luck of the draw . . .
And I'm so tired of hearing that I am strong because of it—
What about all those people with happy lives who manage to screw it up anyway?
I am so tired of being strong . . . hurting so much . . .

The Science of Memory

wondering if there is any end to this . . .
And my eyes hurt and my heart hurts
and the emptiness is pervasive.
And I just want it to stop.

9

Grief

Sunshine crept around the edge of the curtains. Reluctantly, I opened my eyes. Morning again. I stretched myself out of the fetal position. My heart sank as bits of a dream surfaced . . . and this dream hadn't been sweet.

I remember crying in my dreams for many years. The settings changed, but the common thread was that I was weeping in a roomful of people and nobody noticed. Nobody tried to help. Nobody cared. And I wasn't even trying to hide it from them.

Within the dream, I never understood exactly why I was crying. I knew the dreams had gotten worse since I had been diagnosed with dissociation.

This morning I only knew that grief must have taken over that night as I slept.

I met with John a few days later.

"Sunday night I had another crying dream," I told him. "I remember it, but this is too weird—the dream—what happened was I was lying on the kitchen counter and there was sadness and this big guy was there. He was trying to comfort me and getting very close and I kept telling myself, *This is nothing; he's just trying to protect me.* There wasn't really fear, but I felt this twanging going on. It hurts, but I can't define it."

John asked, "What are you sensing?"

"Confusion. It's like, *You don't deserve to be comforted. That's for other people.* And it's a sense of isolation."

John's notes from our early sessions (2002–2003) are full of expressed grief and despair. We (the little ones as well as the adult me) suffered through layer after layer of misery during those years. Hope was nowhere to be found. Italics in the following session notes indicate I am describing what we (a little one and me) are seeing.

John asked me what was happening.

I narrated what was playing on my mental view screen:

Nothing is coming to mind—just this sadness. It's like I'm on the outside looking in. It's like the orphan in the old Dickens tales. They're looking in at all these presents and wonderful things, but they're not a part of it.

So many pictures. Like fathers playing with their kids, married couples caring for each other, people walking hand in hand through a park, all sorts of things. It's really like looking through a window. I can see through but can't get through. And I heard the words, "You're not entitled."

I flashed back on kids teasing and excluding me, saying, "You're not like us. You'll never fit in."

JOHN: What are the feelings associated with all that?

It's ... despair. Hopelessness. Resignation.

I had always wondered why I so rarely felt positive emotions. Then, during one session, God revealed a memory in which the cult had deceived the child by using a cadaver or a mannequin. They shocked its empty chest with an electrical wire to show her it didn't hurt. Only its legs jerked.

Then they shocked me and it hurt. They said it was because I had a heart, and that's where pain comes from.

John asked what I was feeling.

I'm a phony. Feels like it's all just words, like, "I'm the righteousness of God in Christ." It's just words we use to make other people think we're righteous, too.

"So you're just fooling people? You're not really righteous?"

No. We won't ever be.

"Why not?"

'Cause we don't have a heart anymore ... The only thing I keep seeing is this U-shaped thing with nothing in the middle, and that's where the heart should be. And it's not there.

"Holy Spirit, show her what was the lie they taught her there."

The heart's dead but the body still moves, so you don't really need one. If your heart hurts, it doesn't matter.

Manipulating a child is fairly easy. You repeatedly tell her how worthless she is and how great you are. Emphasize that she is nothing without you. She belongs to you. No one else will ever care about her, not like you do. No one will ever believe her if she tells. And, of course, repetitive pain goes a long way toward achieving your goal of confusing her until she dissociates.

John and I unearthed episode after episode of electric shock, drugs, and deception. The child me learned to hate the cult members, men in general, women in general, Jesus, God, and especially herself. Being unable to defend herself, and despising herself for her perceived weakness, she eventually felt she deserved whatever the cult members did.

Then when the memories were exposed, she began to deny what happened.

(the child): I feel like I'm making all this up.

"What about that, Holy Spirit? Can she make up all this emotion and pain?"

That's what they said to do.

"What?"

To make up stories. Because what happened is worse but it didn't really happen. They wanted us to go around in circles. And we can't stop it and we can't finish it 'cause it starts all over again.

"So it's a never-ending story?"

Uh-huh.

Denial became a commonly used defense mechanism but it (unlike confession for a wrongdoing) never eased her anguish. The irresolvable conflict of speaking horrendous truth versus lying about its existence only prolonged the pain.

When you're convinced you are all alone and it will be that way forever, that you'll never fit in anywhere, and that no one cares about you, it's a recipe for despair. That's where the cult wants you, because then you are bonded to them.

Fear prevails. All shreds of hope vanish.

Grief intensifies. Despair overpowers.

It weakens you from deep within your soul, like termites or . . . carpenter ants.

My current, bi-level house had an upper-level landing next to the kitchen door. It was a fine little area to access the back yard. That is, until I realized its four-foot-by-four-foot surface was just too small for me to be able to lounge out there and read. Twelve by twelve feet would be more functional.

Demolition soon began. And I was about to discover what had been happening beneath the wood's surface.

"Yeah," the contractor declared. "It's a good thing you called when you did. That deck is not stable. It's about ready to fall down."

He showed me a damaged piece of wood. I had no idea that carpenter ants had made a home inside the support posts. The trails they'd left behind had honeycombed and severely weakened the wood. I saw the adult ants gathering at the disturbed post's base, and a few eggs were inside.

I could have been seriously hurt had the landing given way with me on it. The only remedy was to tear down and rebuild the deck.

Just as the ants nearly destroyed the landing from the inside, the abuse and its aftermath nearly destroyed me internally. But God had other ideas, ones to give me hope and a future (see Jeremiah 29:11).

Slowly, carefully, He implemented those plans.

Church had always seemed to be the only place I could express emotion of any kind, but especially sadness or grief. Whether it was because of a song or a scripture verse, I felt a little freer to cry.

For a couple of years, I found myself suddenly sobbing uncontrollably during worship. I felt no emotion, none at all. I wasn't sad or lonely, or any of the numerous feelings that can lead to tears. I wasn't even sensing God's presence. I simply doubled over, weeping deeply. And then it would end as abruptly as it had begun.

No one reached to comfort me. I was grateful for that, because what would I say to them?

"Sorry for being a disruption. I don't actually feel bad; it just happened. I have no idea why I was crying."

Virtually every person in the small congregation knew my history. I was surrounded by people who probably understood this weeping was somehow related to my healing. No one ever asked me about it afterward. I wouldn't have had an answer anyway.

Just as I had wept in my dreams for so many years, now I was weeping without emotion in the presence of God's people. But why?

By the time my pastor had resigned and I had moved on, I had gotten less self-conscious about the healing process. I had also begun to understand the underlying issue: grief.

Hard as it was to believe, I was now grieving the despair, loss, and isolation my dreams had exposed. It seemed that a tiny channel to my external landscape had been opened. The grief could finally break through. As in my dreams, it was emotionless expression of emotional pain.

As my counseling sessions continued, I began to understand that the guardians in my mind felt very strong emotions. They actually had a wider emotional repertoire than I did at that point. And they weren't unrelated strangers at all. Although separate, they were all still part of me.

My friend Linda often called her little ones her "very own small group." That's amazingly near to the truth. John and I discovered lots of times that the little ones defended one another as best they could. They also felt pain and grief for the suffering of others. Some expressed anger that they were unable to help those who stayed and took the pain. Sometimes it was like watching a scary movie when the audience screams at the character, "Don't go in there!" The little ones even argued once in a while.

The little ones certainly did talk to one another, and occasionally to me. I often heard them, although it was usually more like static in my mind than clear words. You could call it an office "grapevine." Or a "family discussion."

John commonly asked a little one who was found in the throes of pain or rage if she knew the true Jesus. If she said no, he asked if it was okay to invite Jesus to meet her. Usually, she refused because she had bad memories of a false jesus hurting her. Sometimes she asked more questions about Him to get decision-making information. And when necessary, the ones who had already met Him encouraged her to get to know the true Lord Jesus.

Once her questions had been answered, hesitation dissolved. She agreed to meet the true Jesus. Then He came

Grief

in and ministered love and kindness to her in a way she could understand and receive.

He never pushed or approached without her permission. Never touched her suddenly. Never spoke loudly. He always appeared as a kind and gentle daddy to her. (Although a little one once referred to Him as "Uncle Jesus.")

Just as each of us is a unique individual, each little one was distinctly herself. I believe that's part of the reason why the healing journey took so long. Every time Jesus brought healing, He customized His actions to each one. I watched as He focused His loving attention solely on her as evidenced in the following excerpt:

> JOHN: I command that false jesus to leave now. *(Pause)* Lord Jesus, what do You want to show that little girl?
>
> NARRATOR: *She is crying and grieving.*
>
> John cut the soul ties between the false jesus and the child.[10] Then:
>
> JOHN: Jesus, would You reconcile her with herself? *(Pause)* Is He there with you?
>
> I nodded.
>
> JOHN: What's He doing?
>
> LITTLE ONE: *I'm on His lap.*
>
> JOHN: Just stay right there with Him until He's done. *(Long pause)* Now what's going on?

LITTLE ONE: *He, uh, He's rocking me. And then He showed me we were playing a kid game, and then He started throwing me in the air. And He never dropped me. He's saying I can come to Him with anything and He won't reject me. And He won't say I'm wrong for feeling that way, wrong for feeling something, and He won't belittle me.*

I don't have to hold my "self" together, because He won't let me come apart. Because His arms are stronger than anything else!

And He's saying He won't patronize or placate because He always tells the truth. It's like all I've ever heard were lies, but they weren't from Him. It's because He's not divided. The people, they're all divided. They're divided with hate, but He's pure love.

After repeated incidents of Jesus treating the little ones like the children they were, I realized that I was feeling their emotions in my own life. They were indeed a part of me, and once the walls between us started dissipating, I understood their pain.

I felt it too.

"Contend, oh Lord, with those who contend with me;

Fight against those who fight against me.

Take up shield and armor,

Arise and come to my aid.

Grief

Brandish spear and javelin against those who pursue me;

Say to me, 'I am your salvation.'

May those who seek my life

Be disgraced and put to shame;

May those who plot my ruin be turned back in dismay,

May they be like chaff before the wind,

With the angel of the Lord driving them away;

May their path be dark and slippery

With the angel of the Lord pursuing them.

Since they hid their net for me without cause

And without cause dug a pit for me,

May ruin overtake them by surprise—

May the net they hid entangle them,

May they fall into the pit, to their ruin.

Then my soul will rejoice in the Lord

And delight in his salvation.

My whole being will exclaim,

'Who is like you, oh Lord?'

You rescue the poor from those too strong for them,

The poor and needy from those who rob them."
(Psalm 35:1-10 NIV)

About three years into the healing journey, John read this entire psalm aloud. He called it "The Cry of the Little Ones," and as he read it, I could just imagine Jesus fighting for me against those who would attempt to destroy me to build themselves up.

The following March, I attended a mountain retreat. Outside, the snowbanks were head-high to most of us attendees, and it was bitterly cold. Inside, however, the Spirit of God (and a huge fireplace) provided a warm atmosphere. We all hated to leave.

Most of us met weekly for a neighborhood Bible study; the next one was five or six hours after I returned home. After a well-deserved nap, I dragged my physically weary self to the meeting, anticipating another encounter with the living God.

I got more than I bargained for.

Suddenly my peace evaporated. Anguish hit like a football lineman. I knelt, doubled over, face nearing the floor, weeping and grieving over what I knew was inside me.

Harassing me relentlessly, the enemy lied to me. He shouted that I was damaged beyond repair. My heart despaired. How could I ever get beyond this?

Grief

Sobbing, I cried out to the Lord. "Jesus, You know I would get rid of this stuff if I could." My fingers gripped the edge of the end table. "But I can't!"

This confession was incredibly difficult. I was used to taking care of myself, solving my own problems. But this—this was way beyond my strength and my ability to fix. Did anyone have what it would take to heal me, inside and out? Did God really care?

Then I saw Him. Jesus came toward me. He was riding a white horse, and He was wearing the shiniest silver suit of armor I'd ever seen. It wasn't like the pictures you see of Him coming back to earth, dressed in white robes. If it had been, I would have thought that well-known image was straight out of my own mind.

He was my knight in shining armor? Never saw that one coming!

I continued to watch His approach, curiosity overcoming doubt. Then He stopped. He spoke.

"I am your warrior."

That was all. It was enough. Those four words convinced me that I didn't have to heal myself. I didn't have to attack my problem alone. Jesus was fighting for me. My warrior knight would continue to fight for me until the battle was done. We would get through this together.

And I went from despair to experiencing tiny glimmers of hope. Maybe my internal landscape wouldn't be desolate forever.

10

Identity Theft

"Oh, aren't you a little cutie? Take a look at that nose—it's just like her daddy's."

"She looks so much like her mother. And did you hear that same adorable giggle?"

People say many such things about a child. They generally perceive her to have a family member's best features, whether or not it's true. I've even heard of strangers attributing a parent's characteristics to an adopted child being pushed in a stroller.

It's human nature. And it's generally a good thing. It can help the child grow up with a sense of belonging and identity when these positive remarks are heard repeatedly. Anecdotally, the ratio of five positive to one negative comment is effective in helping the child develop a positive self-identity and good self-esteem.

As I grew up, I often wondered who I looked like. Was I really a part of this family? I even made up a story about being an alien, the kind from another planet. Of course, I didn't fool anybody, not even myself.

Then, in my teens, I noticed I bore a faint resemblance to my maternal aunt. Hmm.

Identity Theft

About seven months after my mom died, I flew out to visit my cousins. Years had passed since I'd seen them after we all grew up and went our own ways. Two of them picked me up at the airport. As I settled myself in the car, the younger one exclaimed, "The first thing I said when we saw you was, 'She looks just like Aunt Janet!'" And when I passed a picture around at the grief support group later that year, one member repeated the sentiment with a comment about "a definite family resemblance."

Yep. Identity confirmed. I was unquestionably my mother's daughter.

Cults know all about identity. They know how to damage the original and they know about creating false ones, all through abusive repetition. They begin by accessing the child in the early stages of identity development. Then negative words, accusations, and lies are efficiently absorbed.

They told me so many lies.
About God:

- *God abandoned you. He won't help.*
- *God has no real power.*
- *He only loves other people, not you.*

About themselves:

- *We hold the power of life and death.*
- *We will always be watching you.*
- *You belong to us. We chose you.*

About myself:

- *You don't have any righteousness.*
- *You're worthless. You can't do anything right.*
- *Who would believe a stupid little girl like you?*

These and multiplied other deceptions formed my false identities and ravaged my feelings about myself. I believed it wasn't safe to be a girl. It was better to be alone than to risk more pain. It would have been better if I had died.

Now add that ugly verbal abuse to the physical abuse I discovered in the session notes. The cult rarely actually hit me—I'm sure they didn't want to leave marks—but a spinning chair, sudden loud noises when they slammed a fist onto the table I lay on, and mild (though painful) electric shocks were regular occurrences.

They also included frequent sexual abuse. Memories of real or threatened rape (often from a false jesus) hurt and terrified me. Ceremonies of false marriage (to demons or cult members); false death, burial, and resurrection (mocking Jesus); and false Communion were all incorporated into the torment.

I'm sure once I learned to dissociate, the abuse decreased somewhat (since the cult could more easily control me) but it never really ended. Cult members continually reinforced the lies and the pain. They also interspersed a few positive comments to keep me off balance.

I continued to form more and more little guardians. Some were complex alters (or, alternate personalities), but most took on only one characteristic and stayed within that role until s/he was released by Jesus.

Identity Theft

ME: *This is really weird. We're right there at the edge of the memory and somebody is there to fling us back again.*

JOHN: Is that a guardian?

ME: *Um-hm. He's got a sword. He's scared. It's his responsibility, his role, but he's too little for that sword.*

JOHN: Holy Spirit, what do You want him to know?

ME: *He doesn't have to hold it anymore, 'cause it's too heavy. He's just a little kid and he can never go play! He doesn't wanna wear the armor anymore—it's too big and heavy.*

Then the tough little guy opened one small latch and the armor fell off, exposing his blond hair. Now he has light shining on him that he never had before. He can go play. No more guarding. And he can give up his false identity.

The little ones didn't only sequester and protect awful memories. They also took on false identities reinforced by the cult while I (the core person) maintained the true identity God created me to have, however damaged that was.

"Executive" was a little guardian who was all business.

JOHN: She's done a really good job protecting.

NARRATOR: *She's saying she had to stay separate, 'cause she's the last fallback position. She's the only one that can pull it all together when it all falls apart.*

JOHN: Is that true, Lord Jesus?

NARRATOR: *She's not gonna listen to Him. She said, "I've seen too much."*

She doesn't bend, fight, or argue. She's just "set." And she's dressed like a businesswoman, in a suit.

Eventually, she met the true Jesus and laid down her responsibility. Then her false identity merged with my true one, adding its uniqueness to my own, where it was intended to be all along.

True identity is that which we were created to be. It is a state of being, not one of doing. For example, my created identities include that of child of God, introvert, female. And the cult tried to steal all three.

All of us struggle with false identities to some degree. True identity comes from the Creator and is innate. False identity comes from outside ourselves and is like an ill-fitting coat. We know somehow it's not truly ours, but we just don't know what to do with it.

I'd only been seeing John for about a year when we dealt with my painful lack of a feminine identity. We had continually discovered how the cult had tormented me through bizarre ceremonies. They'd deceived me into believing their awful lies about my personhood. And I lived with those lies for many years, still believing them until God intervened.

I come from a long line of farmers, so there aren't too many "girlie-girls" in my extended family. My parents came of age during the depression and World War II. Who had time for froufrou?

Mom was a bit of a character who dreamed of becoming a surgeon at a time when women didn't do that sort of thing. From that mindset, she always encouraged me to be who I

was. I shouldn't just try to be what others wanted me to be. But my question remained:
WHO AM I?

God had started preparing me for the healing journey a few years before it began. I got acquainted with Family Foundations, International (FFI) in 1996 when a friend found out about an Ancient Paths I seminar scheduled nearby.

Jan told me everything she knew about it, complete with brochure. "Sounds like it might be interesting, so I'm going. Do you want to come with me?"

I thought about the pros and cons. "You already registered?"

"Yes. And no pressure. It's okay if you don't want to go, but I'll be there. I'll even pick you up if you want."

I studied the material she gave me. I decided to go. And a few days before the seminar, she bailed. The thing is, I'd already paid the registration fee. I hated wasting money (still do!). So I went, not knowing a soul. And not having a clue as to what would transpire.

The leaders, David and Paulette, shared fascinating and inspiring material focusing on the love of God and our identity in Him. These caring facilitators ministered inner healing to each of us attendees through teaching, discussion, and prayer.

I always feel it's pure hyperbole when someone declares, "This thing changed my life." But this seminar actually did. Here's how:

After my father died in the 1980s, I asked Mom where my name had come from. As far as I knew, no one else in the family had that name. She told me the story:

"I felt like you would be a girl, no matter what other people said. If you were a girl, your father wanted to name you Martha. My choice was Cynthia, so I could call you Cindy. We went around and around and never could agree." This was before routine ultrasounds were done during pregnancy.

"So, where did Carolyn come from? A book you read?" Mom had always been an avid reader.

She chuckled as she shook her head. "I was pregnant with you when my father died. He didn't leave a will, and I guess none of the adult siblings wanted the farm. I hated seeing it leave the family, but the law said any property had to be sold and the money split equally among the survivors."

"No will? How come?"

"I'm not really sure. I just know he avoided 'legal things.' Anyway, our estate attorney had a daughter named Carolyn, and your father and I both liked it. Simple as that."

"That's it?"

"Mm-hmm."

So I became Carolyn.

But all my life, I just knew I was supposed to have been a boy. I grew up believing without doubt that I was born the wrong gender. Never really told Mom about it; she'd told me she wanted a girl since she already had my brother. I struggled not to envy him as we played together growing up.

And now I squirmed in my chair as we learned about identity.

Near the end of Ancient Paths, Paulette prayed with me. My defenses went down and she knew it. She leaned in closely to ask, "Carolyn, what's on your mind?"

Struggling to gather my courage, I admitted to her what I'd never told anyone else. Strangely enough, a fellow sitting near me said he had gotten a strong impression (a "God word") of the same thing: wrong gender.

Though I judged myself, Paulette didn't. "Oh, that's all right. God knows who He meant you to be. Just ask Him to show you."

I nodded with a fair amount of uncertainty. How would He answer? Would I even recognize it?

As the seminar wound down, all the participants were given the meanings of our names. Reactions were mixed; some participants were strongly moved, some already knew the meaning, and some were, frankly, confused. This was something new for them to ponder.

For example, Daniel (my brother's name) means "God is my judge".

Well, "Carolyn" means... wait for it... "noble and womanly".

I gasped. My soul quivered at the revelation. God had named me! He'd presented my parents with a wholly different name from the ones they'd been considering.

Now I would be able to know His plan for me. Finally I could know my true identity. Coincidence? I think not.

Although I received this truth with gladness, full healing had yet to come.

2002

My next session with John arrived. We chitchatted per usual, and then the dreaded question: "Ready to get to work?" Time to deal with more pain and the lies that caused it.

I knew the deepest and most fundamental issues were also the most complex. It generally took several sessions in a memory for God to reveal the lies and then to heal my pain with His truth. This was no exception.

They made me climb some steps and lie on the table. Then they put ropes over me.

A deep voice said, "This is a good girl. You won't have to hold her down."

There's a lady at the other end, just barely in the light. She won't help me. She won't even look at me. Why won't she look at me? Am I that bad?

The voice comes again: "Your name is Carolyn but it's a false name. It's a woman's name and we're going to give it to her. You don't deserve that name. You are a liar and you are nothing. This name is one of honor and you have no honor."

(Chanting begins)

And then: *As she was sacrificed for someone else, you have to be sacrificed for her so she can be whole again. You are dead but still alive and she was dead but now is alive.*

Finally: *you will not reach womanhood until we allow it. We own you.* I struggled and then froze as the man put his hand over my mouth and nose. *Your breath will be taken away if you talk about this.*

The cult said my body needed to be separated from my soul. The man in charge declared I would never be like other women. He symbolically drew a knife down the center of my body.

"And now her mind is free to soar, without being weighed down by the rest of her."

He told me, *"Part of you will leave but part of you always stays with us."* Now they owned everything except my mind.

Another lie. As a little child, I believed it. And it remained with me for years.

But, of course, Jesus knew the truth.

A subsequent session returned me to the same memory. More lies and more pain surfaced, which Jesus healed with His love and truth, giving me a bit more peace. But this

Identity Theft

time He also allowed me to experience the function of my smallest alter. The following memory fragment details when Sarah appears for the first time.

> ME: They've never had names before, but I feel like her name is Sarah.
>
> John invited Sarah to interact with Jesus so she could learn to trust Him. I watched them and waited.
>
> Then Sarah spoke: *Can I talk?*
>
> JOHN: You sure can.
>
> SARAH: *I'm the little part that got away when they took the womanhood out of her. He [Jesus] is glad I got away, 'cause I kept what they couldn't take. They thought they could take it but they couldn't take it. I kept it. I did a good job!*
>
> *He says I have a different job now, to talk to the others so they can get to know me 'cause they didn't know me before [pauses and smiles]. I have to go now.*

Little Sarah had one of the most important assignments imaginable: protecting my identity. And Jesus said she did a good job.
Yes, she did.

11

Alters versus Little Ones

"How many personalities did you have?" I can practically see the anticipatory drooling when someone asks me that question. And I just know my answer will disappoint them.

After all, most people have watched stories like *Sybil*, a movie where the main character had twenty-six distinct personalities; *The Three Faces of Eve*, in which the main character had three quite disparate personalities; or *The United States of Tara*, a cable television program featuring a character with multiple personalities. A fair amount of young adult fiction novels on the subject are also available.

I've also seen plenty of television crime dramas wherein the villain is a victim of abuse-based dissociation and of course doesn't know what he or she has done until that personality emerges to tell the story. These dramatic types of presentation are admittedly fascinating, and *Sybil* was based on a true story, but these programs never show you just how diverse the problem of dissociation and dissociative identity disorder is from person to person. They seem to assume that it's the same for everyone. It isn't.

I found my alternate personalities—also called "parts," "alters," or "little ones"—solely during sessions with John.

Since they'd only been appearing when I was dissociated, I was unaware of them before that time. If a part was strong and appeared on a regular basis, John and I believed they could have a name, and we asked about it. I never searched my mind for that name; it was as if the alter told me herself or himself, often without being asked—suddenly I just knew.

Sticking an identity tag on each one simply wasn't all that important. You see, most of the parts had no name. They weren't full-blown personalities. They were just little guardians who protected me from seeing the painful, potentially destructive memories and fears.

The most important thing to remember is that each individual part was valuable. Jesus cherished every single one; none was insignificant in His eyes. I once saw a mental image of Him sweeping tiny golden shards into a barrel. None of them were lost as He searched for and found each one. Some were larger than others, some were crescent-shaped, and some were just specks. By the time He was finished, the barrel was full nearly to the brim.

My authentic self had been shattered like a windshield in a head-on collision; that was true. But Jesus cared deeply, knowing that all those broken fragments were part of the original me He'd created. Just as in the Bible's story of the lost coin (Luke 15:8–10), Jesus was not about to let any of them be forgotten. Even if I didn't know where they were, He did. And He led me to them. He showed them to me so I could understand that they did exist and they were the reason I'd always felt fragmented.

When I was within a memory, the little ones always appeared as children of various ages. They normally guarded the core person against seeing a picture associated with a memory, but when the memory was unearthed, they stepped aside after learning that their job was no longer necessary.

Some of them took a lot of convincing before they would surrender their efforts to Jesus, who was bigger and stronger than they were. Fatigue finally helped them trust Him. I guess you could call it burnout—they were tired of being strong and learned that only Jesus could take care of them. Of course, many had been tormented or betrayed by a false jesus, so they had learned to hate and fear who they thought Jesus was.

Most of the little ones I saw lived and hid in a warren of caves. I saw this place as having a large central area and smaller caves surrounding it, extending to the right. Some of those had a gate or fence to help the little ones feel safer, but some of those gates were broken and askew.

The left aspect of my mental vision was a sunlit meadow. I felt a stark difference as I gazed in my mind from left to right. Then I realized Jesus was in the light, and He would enter the darkness.

The little ones stayed in the dark, frightened and alone. Each seemed unaware of the others at the time, just as a small child thinks no one can see her when she covers her eyes. Light scared them, as did being approached. They feared being touched.

Jesus was very patient and gentle when He entered their realm, and He never did anything without their agreement and permission. He searched them out and rescued them, often leading or carrying them to safety in the sunlight outside the caves. It wasn't unusual for them to grow and become healthy as I watched on my mental viewing screen during the rescue.

No matter how big or mature they were, no matter what job they did, I knew they were parts of my mind that had

Alters versus Little Ones

been formed (split off) for a purpose. And that purpose was important.

When I work with a client now, I often ask what the part wants to be called rather than asking each part's name. This is simply for ease of communication. When the client is speaking through the part (or vice versa), it can be confusing to call them both "Sally." It can be uncomfortable for the client as well as making it harder for her to focus. In addition, asking the question tells the part that I recognize her existence, I acknowledge she is real and that I will listen to her.

Often the name reflects how the part feels about herself (*bad, evil,* and *trouble child* have come up recently). At other times, it seems an arbitrary choice. Sometimes the part expresses no preference; then I just call her "little one" or "guardian." *The important thing is that that part of the mind feels respected after a lifetime of rejection.*

I wish I could convey just how important this is. We know that these are simply parts of the mind and actually part of the person, but because these parts have been acting as protectors, they are just like separate entities. They have their own limited personalities, they speak as children, they are sensitive, and they try hard to do the job assigned to them.

Some survivors hate their own alters. They don't realize that in hating the little ones, they express hatred for themselves. Some rage at the little ones, as though they were rebellious, misbehaving children. This negative behavior often causes more damage, making it harder to reach healing.

Some survivors are so ashamed of being dissociative that they refuse to acknowledge the very existence of parts/little ones. Many dissociatives, of course, haven't yet received the proper training in how to accept and deal with their own parts.

Some therapists believe the ultimate goal of treatment is integration. It really isn't. The genuine goal is healing. When the little ones are ready, they will generally integrate on their own, with or without real-time encouragement. When they meet Jesus and realize He has set them free, they often want to explore and enjoy that freedom for a while. They are children, and they want to play! Forcing them to comply with integration prematurely is not only disrespectful to them but usually unpleasant to the (client) core person.

Premature integration often doesn't last because alters can certainly hide and falsely appear to integrate. Perhaps they feel they need to do what is expected of them. These little ones came into being as a defense against force and coercion through physical, psychological, emotional, and/or spiritual measures. They don't need any more victimization.

John always spoke to the parts as though he were speaking to a child. Sometimes he used a term they did not know (because they were too young to understand) and had to substitute a simpler word. He quickly learned how to interpret my facial expressions. He also consistently offered the little ones a different way to look at something that frightened them. Just as a small child will peek through her fingers or hide behind a wall to look around the edge, the little ones responded to being offered a way of feeling safer.

I was always co-conscious (my presenting, adult self watched internally and knew what was happening) and I would occasionally have to pull out of the alter perspective to explain something to John. Then I returned to being the child alter. I heard myself speak with a child's voice, I perceived having only a child's level of education, and I saw from the child's perspective. I recognized all those things even while the adult me was watching and listening.

I also frequently pulled out of the memory and back into the adult self because the pain and confusion got too intense. Those times became choice points: Would I go back in or not? Honestly, the only logical choice was to keep returning to the memory no matter how painful. How else would I reach healing? Returning was the lesser of two evils. And it was the only one with potential for restoration.

I had four named alters. The smallest was Sarah. She was too young to have experienced much of the torment. She only came out when all the others were "asleep" and then only stayed out for short periods of time. She really liked hanging out with Jesus and was as sweet and innocent as they come. I found myself often speaking her thoughts and feelings because of her limited vocabulary.

The next two were ten-year-old twins named John and Joann. They were defenders. Since John was a male alter, his job was to protect the rest of us with his strength. He was a fighter and rather militaristic. Jesus once presented him with a medal of valor, and was he proud of it! Joann was more of a verbal defender; her weapons were often argument, sarcasm, and debate. She was definitely a take-charge kind of girl and proud of her accomplishments.

The oldest was Beth; she was an adult. I believe she was formed last and matured right along with me. I also believe we often acted in concert when I was only partially dissociated. Beth is probably the main one who took over during my "lost afternoon" at work.

All of my alters seemed to act a lot like me. None exhibited my entire personality since they all participated in my life only in certain specific circumstances. I suppose someone could question whether they were really alternate personalities. However, anyone who paid close attention could tell the difference, as evidenced by Tom, an old friend I visited on vacation some years ago.

Over the years I'd given him regular updates, telling him much of what I went through with my counselors. Tom is a licensed professional counselor, so he was able to understand the majority of what I revealed and to correlate it with his own observations and training.

Tom and I went to see a miniature horse farm located in southern Texas on this hot day in late spring. Wire fences formed corrals, keeping us from getting close to the tiny adult horses. We went to the stables to find out if any foals were out and about. Perhaps we could get a breath of cool air while we oohed and aahed over the adorable babies. We stepped inside and paused to let our eyes adjust to the dimness...

There they were! Two brown foals, one with white facial markings, and one black foal with two white stockings, cuddled with their protective mothers, one by the mangers and the others by the water tank. Such completely delightful youngsters!

Too soon, the caretakers informed us about the dwindling visiting hours. Back out to the heat...

Tom and I found some shade at the edge of one of the corrals. I knelt and wound my fingers through the wire mesh, feeling myself relax just by watching the diminutive, peaceful creatures. A child part seemed to be pushing near my mind. Could she want to say something? She didn't come closer to the surface, but I told Tom about her anyway.

"I have this ten-year-old alter named Joann," I said, not looking at my friend. This wasn't easy to talk about, even with him. "She protects me, but not like her twin, John. He's more of a physical defender, but she's good at verbal defense. You know: sarcasm, cutting wit . . . that sort of thing."

"Yeah, I think I met her a few times," he replied.

A tiny chuckle escaped. "It wouldn't surprise me."

My preferred method of defensive communication for years was sarcasm and argument—I do remember part of that. I also remember being very good at it. Or was that Joann? Or both of us in concert? I used to say I could cut someone up verbally so well they wouldn't even notice until the next day.

The good news is I'm not quite so proficient at it anymore. (Though sometimes I wish I were—oops!)

How can you tell when an alter is active? Often, you can't unless you can catch the quick change of focus in a person's eyes. Some alters are such strong defenders that they act like demons to make people back off. When asked, they might even declare that they are a demon. But they aren't—they are just little ones who are terrified of failing their job assignment. They are petrified about what might happen to the person they are supposed to protect. And they can't be cast out since they are part of the person. They belong there. It's their home.

Even the well-trained and experienced John wasn't always able to differentiate demon from alter. And, yes, once or twice he did try to bind and cast out an alter who appeared to be demonic. It didn't work.

Then he realized the truth: "You're not a demon at all. You're a little one, aren't you?"

"No! I'm a demon! I'm bad and I'll hurt you!"

"I don't think so. I think you're a little one and you're just doing your job, protecting her. And maybe you're a little scared."

"No..." The voice—my voice—softened and lost confidence.

"I'm sorry for trying to cast you out. I was wrong. Will you please forgive me?"

I/she nodded after we thought it over. A grown-up asking for forgiveness was entirely new to us.

"You're very brave. I want you to know I'm proud of you for doing such a good job. And I know Jesus is proud of you too."

"I tried really hard."

"I know you did. But I'll bet you're tired. Such a big job for a little kid."

By the time the exchange was finished, the little guardian had been convinced to turn her job over to Jesus. She learned He was a lot bigger and stronger than she was. Because she gave up her job, she was able to rest. She even cried in Jesus' arms from fatigue and relief. I believe she eventually reintegrated on her own terms and in her own time.

And John and I were able to further pursue the emotions, the memory, the lies, and, of course, the healing.

12

Demons

Horrendous deep darkness encompassed me.
"No! Not again!"

Terror kept the words locked in my mind. Horror kept me from screaming for help. Panic paralyzed me: lying on my back, I literally couldn't move.

They had come back. Faceless shadows hovered near my bed.

Evil emanated from them.

Maybe if I kept completely still, they wouldn't hurt me. If I stayed under the covers, they might think I was still asleep.

I breathed as silently as possible: uncomfortable, but would it be sufficient?

Episode after episode disrupted my sleep, without warning and without pattern, beginning when I was a small child. I yearned to cry out for my parents' help, but fear kept me silent. Would they be safe from this threat? What if they didn't believe me?

I never told my folks about it.

Year after year, the attacks continued. I found no relief, even after I accepted Jesus at age ten. They took a short hiatus but returned with a vengeance.

My Personal Holocaust

Sleep was simply not safe. I consistently fought it as I grew up. But through high school, college, and beyond, I increasingly learned the truth about Jesus' love, power, and authority over the darkness.

In my twenties, an inkling of an idea occurred to me: *Maybe He could help.*

I entered the battle first in my mind, mentally saying, "Jesus, Jesus" over and over again until I fell back to sleep.

Slowly I progressed in my struggle. From speaking Jesus' name in my mind, to whispering it, to saying it softly, I engaged the enemy. For that is what it was—evil, tormenting spirits.

Absorbing more and more about spiritual warfare and authority through my thirties, I finally matured enough to trust myself and my Lord. Anger strengthened me. I found my voice.

"You have no right to be here! I am a child of the King and a believer in Jesus Christ. And by His authority, I command you to leave!" They did, and I went back to sleep.

They came back a few nights later as though to test my resolve. I threatened them with the blood of Jesus, and they left for good. They didn't just fade away; they ran. I could feel it.

By that time I was in my forties.

These episodes had never been benign. I had always remembered them the next morning and beyond, but I was too scared to ask my parents or anyone else about them. I never screamed or yelled in my sleep. I was always fully awake. I never kicked or thrashed around in my bed.

Seeking a definitive answer, I read about night terrors. None of the criteria fit my situation. No, this was something more threatening. This was evil.

Demons

I've heard many times that demons can't possess Christians. That's absolutely correct. To be possessed suggests the person is controlled by the demon.

This long-standing problem is one of semantics, or word meaning. The original Greek word *dianízomai* means not "possessed" but "demonized." In other words, demonic activity torments or oppresses you, or a demonic spirit has the legal right (or ground) to be present somewhere in your soul.[11] (An acquaintance calls demons "cling-ons.")

I was demonized for many years, but never possessed. My spirit fully belonged to Jesus, but my soul was littered with the spiritual, mental, and emotional debris from the abuse.

That litter gave the demonic entities legal ground to stay where they were. Just as a litter-filled alley gets infested with vermin, so my soul became infested with spiritual vermin.

They relentlessly screamed in my mind with hate-filled accusations, with unclean images, and with strong urgings toward suicide. They repeatedly emphasized the lies I had heard from the perpetrators: I was bad and worthless, unloved and unlovable, rejected.

They said I belonged to the cult. If I ever talked about the abuse, I had to kill myself, or they would kill my mother and my sister. Or I would die when they took away my breath.

Yes, those spirits had a right to be there. As a ritually abused child, I had unknowingly agreed with what they and the perpetrators told me. Some of my little ones had made covenants with the spirits, frantically hoping they would keep me safe as they had promised.

They lied. Again.

Multiple books exist that explain the hierarchy of demons, but let's keep it simple. I liken the spiritual vermin to physical vermin:

Small demons, of little power, might be considered as cockroaches. They scatter when the lights come on. Deliverance can usually be accomplished by "following hard" after God (see Psalm 63:8 KJV). Changing the internal atmosphere by prayer, worship, studying Scripture, and not going back to old sin are a few ways to do this. Starving the "cockroaches" and living in the light often makes them leave in search of other habitats. Once they've been exposed, they get scared and don't want to stay.

Medium demons might be thought of as mice. Starving them out is helpful, but most also require some kind of trap. When they are discovered, they tend to obey the command of the believer working in the authority of Jesus. They may argue and grumble that they have a legal right to be there, but once that is taken away, leaving is their only option. And they sometimes leave "droppings" (as mice will), which, once revealed, will also need to be cleaned up.

Large demons are like New York sewer rats: big, mean, and tough to exterminate. They don't own the sewers, they just think they do.

The toughest of these are generational demons. These were invited by one or more predecessors who set up the legal ground for them.

I understand my great-grandfather was a high-level Mason. I have no idea about other ancestors, although Eastern Star (a Masonic auxiliary) is also on the family tree. The lodge members took their vows and oaths, declaring that the consequences of divulging secrets would go down through the generations in perpetuity. Because of that declaration, demons attached to those oaths also had the legal ground to attach to descendants.

When the perpetrators tormented me, those same demons participated. I believe the men called on them and others, and they were able to inhabit the legal ground generated through that action.

Getting rid of demons (casting them out) is not always as easy as it could be. I've heard many ministers say that since Jesus has given us His authority through the power of His blood, we only need to claim that authority and command the demons to leave. They are obligated to obey.

This is essentially true, but a bit limited. I don't know a lot of Christians who sincerely believe they have Jesus' authority and use it appropriately. Perhaps they've never learned this powerful truth. Maybe they feel they don't deserve or haven't earned it because of personal sin. Or they simply feel inadequate against the powers of evil. Unprepared, frightened, ignorant; each of these circumstances can be changed by faith and by cultivating intimacy with God.

Scripture tells us about a boy who was tormented by an evil spirit that made him throw himself into the fire and the water. The disciples could not cast it out (see Mark 9:17-29). Perhaps they had allowed complacency resulting from previous successes to creep in, because Jesus told them, "This kind only comes out through prayer and fasting" (v. 29, paraphrased).

The authority is indeed ours, through Christ, but must be cultivated as we follow God's voice. If we rely on our own strength to remove a demon, it may not go. It will recognize our hesitation. It may even react to our lack of commitment to Christ and defy our command (see Acts 19:13-17).

June 2003

The cult had perverted the meaning of Scripture: "Behold, I am with you always, to the ends of the earth" (Matthew 28:20, paraphrased) meant that the cult and the demons would always be present with us.

John asked, "Anything else, Holy Spirit?"

> *It's like a shield or something, and it's propelled by two flying angels. They carry it around my head. And they're black and ugly, and they're all bent.*

JOHN: Anything they must disclose, I command they disclose it now!

DEMONIC ENTITY: She agreed!

JOHN: Agreed to what?

DEMONIC ENTITY: Not reach God.

JOHN: Anything else you have to disclose before you leave?

DEMONIC ENTITY: Not trust God, not worship God. God gives pain.

We broke this false covenant. The demons left because the legal ground was removed.

July 2003

John prayed, "Lord Jesus, would You go in and cleanse the temple? We cut every soul tie by the power of the Holy Spirit, and I bind every unclean spirit and perverse spirit together and cast them out in Jesus' name. [*pause*] Now, Lord, are there any covenants or agreements she needs to break?"

> LITTLE ONE: I don't understand. It's too confusing.

> John took authority over confusion and any spirits causing it, commanding them to give their reason.

> DEMON: *She broke her vow and it got worse. Breaking the vow is worse than all the rest.*

The demons left when John commanded them to go wherever Jesus sent them.

January 2008

One of the little ones had taken on a demonic guardian and was now pumping out anger and fear toward God.

> LITTLE ONE: *It feels like there's a boxing match inside! We don't know what we're fighting. We can't stop. It's too big. We can barely hold it back! It'll take over!*

Jesus was invited to join us as I watched the little one.

LITTLE ONE: *It's big and black and blobby. And he wants to get out and hurt us. He's too big and too scary and too strong!*

Jesus, I'm afraid you won't back me up. I need to see You and know that You're there.

JOHN: Lord Jesus, what's the truth here?

LITTLE ONE: *Every time we stop to listen for Jesus the other one roars and it's so scary and we can't hear and it hurts our ears.*

JOHN: You can tell it to be quiet.

LITTLE ONE: *Ohhhh. Okay. In the name of the true Lord Jesus, we don't want you here anymore. And I command you to stop roaring and be silent. (pause)*

LITTLE ONE: *Jesus roared back at him and put him in a box!*

June 2005

Joe and Sara King had come to hold a three-day seminar titled "Freedom from Freemasonry." Twenty-plus participants made for close quarters in the basement of this private home.

Most of our time was spent in reading Masonic renunciations and praying. We broke curses and vows. We repented for the sins of our ancestors and cleansed our family lines. In short, a complete generational purification took place as we removed all demonic rights within our lineages over that long weekend.

Joe agreed to pray for me at the follow up church service three days later. This would be my last chance for personal ministry since he and Sara were about to return to England.

But I had volunteered to help pray for people! The service was winding down when I finally was free to approach him.

"Remember you said you'd pray for me?"

"Oh, I did. Let me finish this one thing and I'll be right back."

I stood right there, waiting for Joe's return and preparing myself for whatever God had planned.

Joe never asked me what I needed, but he did ask God. Then he put his hands on my shoulders and prayed. Holy power buckled my knees. I fell to the floor.

The next thing I knew, Joe had recruited half a dozen members of the prayer team to surround me. Because I was lying on my back, they were all I could see. But I could hear! Their combined voices insistently commanded the demon(s) to leave. They declared freedom over me and affirmed that no more legal ground remained. They reminded me to join in the battle for my freedom.

My voice barely worked. My waist felt attached to the floor. My torso repeatedly rose and fell, as though I were doing crunches beyond my control.

I gathered my strength. "Get out! I don't want you! Leave or face the blood of Jesus." These were strong spirits who had been in my family line for generations. They would not go willingly.

Twenty minutes passed.

I crumpled as they finally released me. I felt it. The sensation of freedom overwhelmed me as I rolled over and started laughing, my waist at last separated from the floor.

Jane grinned at me. I hadn't noticed my friend engaging the battle with us. I didn't know she had protected my head as I went down onto the concrete floor.

Now we laughed together, she with joy and me with relief. It was over!

We both remember that night.

I also remember that I lay on the couch and wept every evening for a solid week. Emotionally and physically exhausted but spiritually elated, I found that my relief and gratitude for deliverance demanded expression.

November 2023

I got severely triggered while perusing my old session notes, so badly that it felt like an impending panic attack. Rather than giving me ideas on what to include in this book, it paralyzed me. I couldn't even think about writing.

Time to see my counselor for a "tune-up."

The Lord took me back to an old memory that I thought had been thoroughly processed. There I discovered a never-unearthed, deep lie. Within it, I was surrounded by the perpetrators, feeling smothered by them pressing in on me.

NARRATOR: they said, *We're always watching.*

> *Then they dispersed to stand with their backs against the opposite wall, still keeping their eyes on me.*
>
> *They hadn't been the only ones pressing in on me. Demonic entities crowded around.*

Demons

I (the person present in the counselor's office) felt my shoulders drawing in, pulling away from the pressure. I curled up in the chair. I heard myself speaking in a child's voice.

JOHN: Holy Spirit, what does she need to know about these guys?

ME: *It's so creepy. I can feel them closing in.*

We invited the true Jesus to enter the memory. He stood right in front of me, a reassuring presence. I wasn't alone with the tormentors anymore.

LITTLE ONE: *Now that He's here, maybe the rest of them will leave.*

Several of the entities disappeared.

LITTLE ONE: *Jesus took my hand.*

A dozen dark and faceless shapes remained, still pressing on me.

JOHN: You should tell them to leave. You have Jesus' authority.

LITTLE ONE: *I'm going to hold His hand while I do that.*

And I used the authority of Jesus as we held hands. I told them, "In the name of the true Lord Jesus Christ, who is with me, I tell you guys to get out of here and never come back. I don't want you. All of you!"

The demons went, but not before flinging one final lie at me. They showed me their ugly, twisted faces and told me that when people look at me, they see them.
Not so.
Jesus and I started walking.
"Where are we going?"
"Into the light."
And we went, Him and me, still holding hands.

13

False jesus

A child begins to individuate after birth; the baby gradually learns that she is an individual and not just part of her mother.

By the age of eighteen months, the child begins to experience complex emotions. Her ability to trust in herself grows.

By the age of eighteen months, the cults begin to program the child. If all goes well, she learns to survive the torment by turning her mind away from it.

Just when self-confidence is growing, her little heart receives another blow. It never seems to end. But she needs to trust! What else can she do?

And the cult obliges that inborn need. But who are the cultists encouraging the child to trust? The One who is trustworthy above all: Jesus.

Oh, but not the true Jesus; they have their own version of him.

March 2003

> JOHN: Lord Jesus, is there something she needs to know about surviving?

ADULT PERSONA, TRANSLATING FOR THE LITTLE ONE: *If you can't feel it, they can't really hurt you. We won't think about it now; we'll think about it later. That's the only way to do it.*

JOHN: Lord Jesus, what about that?

LITTLE ONE: *He helps them. He's part of them. He works with them.*

JOHN: What does he look like?

LITTLE ONE: *It seems like he's just a guy. He's dressed like they are. His eyes are cold, and he's smiling but it doesn't get to his eyes. They said he was Jesus.*

Why should cultists be interested in getting the child to trust in Jesus? Isn't He the one they fear and despise? Unfortunately, even Satan knows Scripture. Matthew 19:14 says, "Let the little children come to me and do not hinder them, for the kingdom of heaven belongs to such as these" (NIV).

Children in the clutches of the cults know instinctively that Jesus is the only One who can help them. They want to trust Jesus. And the cults are happy to oblige.

During World War II, the Nazi doctor Josef Mengele perfected a horrendous tactic. He knew children are easily fooled and can be manipulated through trickery. If they trust someone, whether a parent, a guardian, or some other type of authority, they (figuratively and/or literally) will fling themselves into the arms of that person for protection.

During his infamous reign, the "Angel of Death" learned that if he presented himself as a glasses-wearing,

False Jesus

kindly doctor, he could engender trust in the child. Then he would turn around and present himself as a barefaced ogre, terrifying the same child. Repeated exposure to this demonic ritual caused the child to dissociate. The unresolvable conflict between the good and the evil being in the same man overwhelmed them.

The cults soon borrowed from Mengele's research. They modified it and used it in evil ceremonies in which they terrified and programmed small children.

The children called on "Jesus," and he would help them, or so they thought. They learned well the lessons of self-preservation.

It's like a fiendish costume party. A member of the cult is chosen or volunteers to portray Jesus for the child. He stands nearby, reassures the child, and encourages her belief in him.

"Do you trust me, Suzie?"

She nods her head, hoping against hope that her pain and her fears will soon be relieved by the one who says he is Jesus.

Once he gains her confidence, he changes. He steps away, crosses his arms, and leans against the wall as though nothing bad were occurring. "Jesus" doesn't care.

Often he participates in the torment. He leers at her and convinces her that she deserves all the pain the cultists inflict. She is bad. She is evil, or even worse, her left side is evil and the right side is good. She must be punished.

He tells her that that God hates her and the only ones who don't are the cultists. He says they only hurt her to make her better.

The lies are intended to emotionally dismantle her.

At first, she fights. She kicks and screams. But eventually, the cultists wear her down. "Jesus" speaks soothing words in her ear and tells her it's good for her to go away. Then she can stop the pain. But "going away" doesn't mean she leaves with a trusted adult. It means she dissociates. Her mind learns how to divide itself to sequester the horrendous memories of what she has survived physically.

At that point, cult members can begin programming her in their own image. She isn't allowed to be little Suzie anymore. Now she is the property of the cult.

This can't be real. No, no, it never happened.

This is wrong. I let him do what he wanted, but it's wrong. But it's Jesus. How can it be wrong? And if it never happened, why does it feel so bad?

I'm as evil as they are. Even God can't forgive me. I'm gonna be in the dark always!

April 2003

Someone, a little one, is holding back.

JOHN: Can I speak to the one that's holding back?

LITTLE ONE: *Don't let her hurt anymore.*

> *He lied to us, lots of times. He said he wouldn't hurt us but he did. A man in a beard and robes. And somebody said he was Jesus.*

JOHN: Holy Spirit, would you show her who that really was?

LITTLE ONE: *He was part of them. He was a liar. He wanted to hurt us. He just pretended to be nice. He wasn't nice. Everybody lies!*

False jesus

I'm all alone. I'm always all alone. It's always been like that. They gave me a comforter, but he really wasn't for me. I was still all alone. You can't trust anybody. The only one to protect you is you.

The comforter said, "Nobody knows you're here. I'm the only one on your side. God can't even reach you here. This is a dark place, and He doesn't come into dark places."

Everybody wants to hurt you. They pretend they don't, but they really do. Don't let down your guard or they'll hurt you more. You gotta protect yourself.

The physical false jesus is bad enough. The torment he causes is horrendous. But there is another type of false jesus—the one on the spiritual plane.

January 2004

> JOHN: Holy Spirit, is that the true Lord Jesus who came in the flesh?
>
> ADULT PERSONA: (She shook her head.)
>
> LITTLE ONE: *He doesn't want us to get fixed. He stands over there watching with his arms crossed. Like this was nothing.*
>
> JOHN: Holy Spirit, would you show her what he looks like?
>
> LITTLE ONE: *There's no face. Just all white, fuzzy, nothing.*

My Personal Holocaust

JOHN: I take authority over that one, and command you to kneel at Jesus' feet.

LITTLE ONE: *He did it. He's kneeling in front of Jesus.*

JOHN: Now, would you like to invite the true Lord Jesus in and see what He looks like?

The little ones nodded and then waited.

LITTLE ONE: *He's soft, and He's not loud. And there's tears on his face.*

JOHN: Why are there tears on His face?

LITTLE ONE: *For us! The other one never had any tears.*

JOHN: No. He was a phony!

LITTLE ONE: *This is all so convoluted. I can't deal with it. We just know it's not safe. We can't even trust us.*

JOHN: Holy Spirit, who can they trust?

LITTLE ONE: *No, we can't trust Jesus 'cause he hurts us.*

JOHN: Holy Spirit, would you show them who that "Jesus" really is?

LITTLE ONE: *We can't see him.*

JOHN: Do you have your eyes closed? You're going to have to open your eyes to see him.

False jesus

LITTLE ONE: *He's all gray and knobby.*

JOHN: Not really Jesus, huh?

Staring cautiously, we shook our head.

Evil spirits are great impersonators. Have you ever had a thought that seemed like a good thing but turned out to be completely the opposite? We all have. And it isn't always from our own minds. It could have been a thought suggested by a clandestine spirit. Evil spirits can't read our minds, of course, but making suggestions is their specialty.

Time after time during our sessions, John would invite Jesus into the memory and He would come. I usually recognized Him immediately. Of course, the little ones who hadn't yet met Him were curious or even afraid of this (to them) strange man. For them He would stand in the distance and let them get used to His presence before approaching. He never pushed, never rushed, and never frightened them. He waited patiently while they watched Him from between their fingers or around a fence.

I often asked myself why the true Lord Jesus would allow an impersonation to occur. Shouldn't He come when invited?

In going through numerous sessions, I learned that Jesus wouldn't come if

- the little one feared or hated him, or if she blamed Him for what she had gone through:

    Will He hurt me?

JOHN: *No, He won't hurt you. Is it okay if He comes a little closer?*

Yeah. This is weird. I can't see His head anymore. When He came closer to the stairs I couldn't see His head.

JOHN: *Holy Spirit, is this the true Lord Jesus?*

I'm afraid to see His face. He might be angry.

- Or because she made a covenant with the false one:

JOHN: *True Lord Jesus, would you reveal Yourself and get rid of that false jesus?*

He's still there.

JOHN: *Why?*

We asked him to protect us 'cause we were so little.

- Or maybe it was because the child expected to perceive Jesus as dark and faceless, as though he had turned away from her like the fake (human) jesus did.

But at other times, an evil spirit would impersonate Jesus. That name may have been assigned to it in the spiritual realm or it may simply have been trying to torment the child into more confusion and dissociation.

When working within a memory, there were a couple of ways to tell the true Jesus from a false one. Simply being in

False Jesus

the presence of the true Jesus made the adult me feel safe, protected, and loved. The little ones all responded in the same manner after they met Him. Sometimes we asked the ones who knew who He was to introduce the others, and they were happy to do that.

The other way was to look at His face. Most of the time, demonic entities pretending to be Jesus were essentially faceless. They appeared in my mind as dark shapes without facial features. No eyes, no expression. I could often feel hatred emanating from them, but I believe the Lord might have had them appear like this to avoid further frightening the little one.

John would ask what this jesus looked like. And when I said I couldn't see his face, John commanded the entity to show his face to me. At that point the false jesus turned away or took off. Sometimes I saw a distorted and angry visage, soon to be replaced by the true Lord Jesus and His loving and kind appearance.

> LITTLE ONE: *He said He was proud of me, but I don't think He means it. He's angry.*

> John invited the true Lord Jesus to come into the memory.

> LITTLE ONE: *I don't want him to trick me.*

> JOHN: He will do whatever you want.

> LITTLE ONE: *Okay. Stay away but talk, okay?*
>
> *He came down a slope but He's out of arm's reach, so He can't touch me. He's smiling at me—nobody*

ever smiles at me. He said, "You done good"; then He laughed. "You saw what had to be done and you did it, and I'm very proud of you!"

Only rarely did the true Jesus appear to me without invitation, choosing compassion over formality. This episode took my breath away:

John prayed for guidance and grace while I submitted my heart and mind to the Lord. We waited for Jesus to bring a memory to the surface. It soon appeared, clearly and in detail.

I entered the scene, becoming the young child again. This day I felt myself lying on my back on a cold metal table. Several men surrounded me, seen only as dark figures standing there. Threatening and frightening figures. I didn't know what would happen. I did know I didn't want to be there.

Let me go! I want to go home!

The men ignored my pleas and tears. They would do what they wished. They held all the power.

I struggled briefly but found no escape and certainly no pity. I heard myself whimper.

The men spoke softly. I couldn't recognize any of their words. Maybe if I could understand them, it would prepare me for what was to come. I closed my eyes and tried to stop crying. Tried to be brave and to listen.

I finally heard someone speak clearly, but this Voice was not what I had expected.

"Look to Me."

How could anyone sound so gentle, yet so commanding? How could trust be summoned with only three words?

False jesus

I opened my eyes and looked up. Somehow, I looked past the group of men, past the ceiling, past the sky. I looked straight into heaven.

Jesus stood there—and He looked at me. Not through me, as the men did. Not a dismissive glance. A riveting, unwavering gaze.

Our eyes met. His face filled my vision. I no longer saw the men or the room. Nothing but His face and those eyes. It almost felt as though I could fall into them.

My physical and emotional pain faded to nothingness. The fear vanished. His eyes held only love and strength. He infused me with that strength so I could survive the ordeal.

I still knew the evil men were doing something to me, but it was too far away for me to perceive. My body was on earth, but I was connected to heaven and to the One who created all things.

Jesus didn't speak again. He didn't have to. His eyes said it all.

He loved me. He was there for me.

My own strength was gone, but His was sufficient.

14

Why

About half an hour remained before I had to leave for my appointment with John, so I went over the notes from my previous session.

Notes that again exposed what had been done to me by the lodge members.

I tried to work up a tirade, but just couldn't. There were only vestiges of anger when I knew I should have felt serious rage. I'll bet other girls would have. Mostly I just felt . . . exhausted.

One question dominated my mind: Why in the world had these men done those things to me?

I wondered if my capacity for rage was drained from surviving all this, not to mention reliving parts of it for healing purposes. At least I could ask John about it when we met.

"Why? What could I ever do to deserve this?"

John sighed. "You existed. And you fit their criteria. It was nothing you did."

That stirred some pique. "Wait a second. Are you saying I was—what?—handy?"

I could feel my muscles start to tighten, my jaws to clench. I tried to relax but managed minimally. Deep breaths shuddered. How could those men have been so incredibly cruel?

Silence reigned for a few seconds. I grabbed a tissue, wiped away tears. My racing heart slowed a bit. Maybe it was enough. I was sort of ready to listen.

John cleared his throat. "In a word, power."

"Power?" I hadn't expected that. What did that even mean?

"Yes. Cults want it and will do anything to get it."

My mind flitted and zoomed, searching desperately for a coherent thought. "What kind of power? I mean, sure, they had power over me. I was just a kid."

Agitation. My foot wouldn't stay still. Changing position helped.

"We've talked about cults using trauma-based mind control and dark spiritual power."

"Yeah." Tears burned my eyes. "But to do this to a little kid! Why?"

Tears shone in John's eyes, blinked away quickly. He scrolled through his laptop. "Let's start here. Remember this?"

As I read through the note, my soul went back to the child. To the memory of torment, though I knew I would not be re-traumatized.

I knelt in a rectangle barely large enough to hold my small body. Metal strips formed the border. I faced a semicircle of portraits and statues. They represented various and disparate religious figures: Buddha, Vishnu, Jesus, Kali, and others.

"Choose!" the men commanded. "Which is the true god?"

Every time my knees touched the metal strips, an electric shock jolted me. They wouldn't let me be correct.

But their plan succeeded. Through this and other bizarre ceremonies, the spiritual doors were opened. I could now be pushed through at will. The cultists could torment me on both the physical and the spiritual planes.
Power.
Over the years, I had been taught that the spiritual and physical planes exist simultaneously. I always likened the reality to parallel universes, à la *Stargate SG-1*. I know, I know: I'm a sci-fi nerd. It does help me understand the unexplainable.
As does this: my family moved out of state when I was nearly three years old. The odds of being accessed physically dropped dramatically. I should have been out of the cult's reach.
However, the spiritual world is every bit as real and accessible as the physical.

In accordance with their tradition, the ceremonial room was darkened. Shadows flitted. The only things I could clearly see were glowing red eyes within a huge charcoal-gray figure. I felt the men standing behind me, heard them chanting.

They offered me to Satan.

A terrifying, deeply resonant voice slithered into my ears. His reply?

"She will bear me many fine children."

I was about ten or eleven years old, the age of puberty, and certainly not physically present for them. My grandfather had died over a year earlier, so he couldn't have had a hand in this one.

This memory terrified me as much or more than remembering the painful physical encounters.

John asked, "Do you want to bear him children?"

"No!" I exclaimed.

"Tell him."

By this time, I knew John would be spiritually supporting my forthcoming declaration. I had learned my authority in Christ. I understood the blood of Jesus hurt and frightened Satan and his minions.

"In the name of the true Lord Jesus, and by His blood, I reject you. I will not bear children for you. I will only follow Jesus and do His work. I am a child of the King."

Although the memory left me shaken, the intense fear vanished. The anger remained.

Spiritual torment is very real, and the emotional damage causes invisible, lasting scars. Only Jesus has the power to heal them.

Later, John and I discussed mental programming over coffee. "Do you remember *The Manchurian Candidate*?"

I shook my head.

"It's an old movie about mind control. I caught a rerun on TV a few days ago. People were programmed to follow murderous commands while the programmers remained unknown and safe."

My voice wavered. "But that's just a movie, right?"

"Truth-based. Programming's been happening for a lot of years. It's called brainwashing for a reason. Programmers damage or even replace a person's self-identity. And don't forget 'deprogramming' for those who escape the cult.

"The Masons may have tried to program you for who knows what. The fact that you got away could have prevented their success. I don't know."

At last. Something John didn't know. I could relate to that.

"Do you think they tried to program me?"

"You'll have to ask God about it."

Honestly, I hated when he said that. I didn't want to seek out an answer. Too much work!

But no one else was going to do it, so I did. After gathering lots of evidence, I finally came to a tentative conclusion: maybe the Masons had tried to program me to take down ministers and/or churches. It seemed odd that all this and more could have happened within the span of eight years and at three different churches in two different states without some sort of perverse plan:

- a senior pastor whose wife left him, so he had to resign his position
- an associate pastor who tried to take over the large church where he was on staff
- an ex-pastor who tried to rape me

I had been in pastoral counseling with each one.

Oddly enough, all these things and others happened before I truly grasped not only my identity in Christ but how to handle spiritual warfare and demonic attack. Although much of this was simply head knowledge, it still protected me. And, quite possibly, those with whom I worshipped.

The entire concept of ritual abuse blows me away. I can't imagine trying to program anyone to mindlessly do your bidding.

The operative word here is "imagine." The human imagination originated with God. He created us in His image, which means we are also creative. But remember what happened with Satan? As Lucifer, the created angel of light and music, he was beautiful and brilliant. He was loved. He was "Light Bearer."

He wasn't worshipped.

But he wanted to be equal with God (see Isaiah 14). He imagined being in that role, not satisfied to be himself. That imagining took over his existence as he recruited other angels into his rebellion. Trust no longer existed, and God cast them all out of heaven. Now they influence mankind toward evil.

The perpetrators imagine they can be gods. To that end, they perform a myriad of ceremonies. They speak curses and make vows that affect not only them but their families for generations. They torment and abuse children.

Some cults imagine they will absorb the life essence of the child through sex and thereby prolong and enrich their own lives. Some openly court demonic entities to join them and then implant those demons into the children.

All for power.

I can't wrap my mind around the concept that they think this is all a good thing. You can't either, can you?

Here's why.

In Philippians 4:8, Paul tells us to think on "whatever things are lovely . . . are pure . . . are of good report" (NKJV paraphrased). When we fill our minds with the things of God, we increasingly become more Christlike. We move further away from evil as it fades from our thoughts.

The reverse is also true. Those who fill their minds with evil become evil. They can't help it. And once you start in that direction, it's hard to stop.

It can be like an addiction.

People don't just get out of bed some morning and decide to become addicted to drugs. It starts slow and grows from there:

A person needs pain medication for a back injury. It eases the pain. Sleep improves; the body heals. But in some individuals, the nervous system sends signals: I need more! Give me more! And in response, the person increases his intake in an effort to repeat that first jolt of pain relief. The cycle starts. More drugs do not equal more relief, but the cravings are quelled for a bit.

Addiction of any type occurs as evidence of the law of diminishing returns. And it continues as long as there is no intervention. That particular law tells us that evil begets more evil in order to satisfy the heart's desires (see Romans 1:18–32). The Passion Translation (TPT) says it this way: The evil "are senseless, faithless, ruthless, heartless, and completely merciless. Although they are fully aware of God's laws ... they still go headlong into darkness" (vv. 31–32).

The King James Version says God has given them over to "a reprobate mind" (v. 28 KJV). The thesaurus gives us updated meanings for this antiquated term *reprobate*: "debased," "immoral," "corrupt," "wicked." It's a long list.

But they all mean the same thing.

Evil.

"Oh, come on. My grandfather was a really good guy. And he was a Mason." I've heard variations of this many times, even within my own family.

Why

Although fewer than fifteen percent of initiates reach the highest Masonic levels where ritual abuse is practiced, the evil has to start somewhere. In this case, lower levels seem innocuous. And respectable people participate. They think it's all good, clean fun. Secret, sure, but so what? Some even give up on the Lodge in boredom after discovering there are no heinous ceremonies discussed at the lower levels.

However, when initiation occurs, the newbie states, "I walk in darkness and seek the light." He is blindfolded (the "hoodwink") and is led around the lodge by a noose around his neck (the "cable tow"). Often, he is allowed to stumble. Then the vows start. Curses are spoken.

But whose darkness are the cultists talking about?
And whose light?

From the beginning, they speak words of destruction and death. The vows they take are curses that affect not only the initiate but his family and descendants.

Until, somewhere down the line, someone calls a halt.

> LITTLE ONE: *It's grandpa's house. He picks up the phone and hears something and gets this look in his eyes. It's like he knows what he has to do and doesn't want to, but he knows he has to.*
>
> JOHN: How's that make you feel?
>
> LITTLE ONE: *I don't know. Despair, maybe.*
>
> JOHN: Holy Spirit, why are You showing her this?
>
> LITTLE ONE: *We're all trapped. I see generations backward and we're all trapped. Nobody can get free.*

JOHN: Holy Spirit, why? Why can no one get free?

LITTLE ONE: *They're too strong. They have too much power.*

JOHN: What's giving them the power?

LITTLE ONE: *Evil!*

JOHN: Holy Spirit, what do You want to show her about that? Is that the truth?

ADULT PERSONA: *I just flashed on my grandmother on my mother's side. And she's praying, and it's like there's a wedge driven into the chain.*

JOHN: What else does she need to see there?

ADULT PERSONA: *I just keep hearing, "It ends here!" And I see a little girl, and she's really, really strong. Not physically but inside, and she's saying, "It ends here!"*

This revelation spoke volumes to my heart. God knew what was happening, and He gave my grandmother the strength to intercede for the family and for me.

Strength to call a halt to the chain of iniquity.

And so, we come to the hardest "why" of all: *Why did God let this happen?*

Man, did I wrestle with that. One day, in one of our many sessions, I finally asked John about it. "Why in the world does God allow this?"

I had a feeling I already knew the answer.

"Free will."

"Excuse me?"

"God gave mankind free will at creation."

I frowned. "I know that. So?"

"When Adam and Eve sinned, they made a choice. They wanted to be like God, 'knowing good and evil' [Genesis 3:5 KJV]. They believed lies from Satan."

"Well, that is his job."

"Not just his job but his character: '*a liar and the father of lies*' [see John 8:44]. Anyway, bad guys have free will and choice as much as good guys. And God won't work contrary to His character. He's the One in charge, but He's not in control of anything we don't give Him control over. He won't take control from you. He doesn't want robots; He wants our free will worship and obedience."

1995

You may have noticed by now that God often speaks to me in pictures.

A few years before the PTSD made itself known, I saw myself standing on a cliff, maybe a foot from the edge. Something like a speed bump was at my feet. If I stumbled at all, over I would go into the deep chasm. I would die.

As I listened to the silence and felt the wind on my face, fear gripped me. I couldn't move an inch. Then a voice said, *"I can't take you any further until you turn everything over to Me."*

Sometimes preachers had encouraged (or threatened) the congregation with this concept. I knew it wasn't possible for me. I didn't want to tell God I would give Him everything and then take it back. How hypocritical would that be?

I wrestled with this for several weeks. Even talked to a counselor friend of mine once or twice. I just couldn't set myself up for failure.

Then God directed my attention to Genesis 15. There, He declared promises to Abram, telling him about his future offspring and homeland (vv. 5–7). Abram brought the animals as God had commanded and prepared them for sacrifice, driving away the birds of prey (v. 10). Then he fell into a deep sleep while God Himself cut the covenant. And though Abram was literally unable to join the process, God would keep both sides.

By illustrating this, it seemed He understood I was only human and therefore fallible. Would He do the same for me?

A few more days of soul-searching and I was ready. "Okay, God. I don't understand, but here goes. You know I'm going to fail, and You accept that. I give You everything. You know me better than I know myself, so You'll have to take over. I can't do it." Done.

Deep sigh. I hated to think of failing. What now?

A few days later, God showed me the cliff again. Same vista, same speed bump, same perspective. But this time, Jesus waited on the other side, visible from the thighs up. Surely, he wasn't hovering in midair. What could He be standing on?

He held out his hand. It reminded me of the old westerns, when the sheriff helps a lady down from the stagecoach.

Filled with curiosity and a bit of trepidation, I took Jesus' hand as He helped me step forward. I looked down to see He was standing on solid ground about eighteen inches below the cliff edge. What I thought was a deadly height was nothing to fear. His strong hand steadied me as I stepped down to stand beside Him.

Jesus expected me to be unable to fulfill the covenant. His only request was that I be willing to try.

At that moment, I freely gave Him control over the whole of my life.

Have I ever taken it back?

Yep. He honors my free will.

Has He ever forgotten or canceled the covenant?

Nope.

A covenant is not a contract. A covenant is for life.

15

Healing Love

Ever hear this one: "Time heals all wounds"? All together now: *Bah!*

Of course, time doesn't heal all wounds. Doesn't heal very many, actually. The body, with enough time, heals numerous physical wounds, but the inner ones? Nope.

It's a bit like storing food in your refrigerator. Things you don't want at the time gradually get pushed to the back. You forget about them being there at all.

Then, when you decide it's time to pull them out, wham! They've turned to concrete. Or a mushy mess. Or maybe penicillin. And let's not even mention the smell.

Nonphysical wounds are comparable. If you forget about them, whether consciously or subconsciously, they morph into something unexpected. No healing there!

I waited more than forty years for my inner wounds to begin to heal. Time didn't heal them. Everything was repressed and buried, just like those refrigerator leftovers. Time made them worse.

Guess what did heal them: love.

So, with all the confusion in our world, let's define love's two predominant types. We have *agape,* or God's full-time, unconditional love. We also have *fileo*, or human, brotherly, often conditional love. Both are necessary for our healing.

In *Living from the Heart Jesus Gave You*, the authors describe what they call Type A and Type B wounds occurring in childhood.[12] Type A refers to the absence of good things you should have received, like unconditional acceptance and lots of hugs. Type B refers to bad things that happened to you through no fault of your own, like abuse in any form. Both types cause lasting damage.

Like so many others, I had both types.

Most churches and counselors are willing and able to help with Type B wounds. Congregations have any number of people with B wounds. Support groups welcome the addicts, the grieving, and those with a variety of other expressed needs. This healing, according to the authors, can be amazingly quick, because B traumas often cover just one event and a comparatively brief span of time. Those people are prayed for, counseled, accepted, and healed. Witnessing their healing encourages others.

But people with Type A trauma wounds are not generally encouraged by this but are continually disappointed. Depression deepens.

What's wrong with me? they think. *Haven't I waited long enough? Or repented enough? Or read the Bible enough?* They wonder if they are just too bad for redemption, or if their painful wounds are too deep for true healing. They may not actually know what caused the Type A wounds, which adds hopelessness to the mix.

Unfortunately, things only get worse when others treat them as if they were B trauma people. In those cases, the feeling of isolation and rejection grows because the community that should have been involved in healing their Type A wounds never recognized them.

No, this healing journey is definitely not "one size fits all."

God's love comes directly from Him, but it also comes through His people. And that takes a community. Spiritual adoption, if you will. I was blessed to have several communities I became part of along the way. Some existed for only a short time, maybe a few days; others lasted for many years. Longevity doesn't matter quite as much if depth is there and if truth and love reign.

A few of the people in each population accepted me for who I was, wounds and all, and then helped me progress toward healing.

The peculiar thing is I usually hated it. I found those people really annoying. I didn't discover why that was true until much later (actually, I reread *Living from the Heart Jesus Gave You* in research for this book). It seems that when someone loves you with a joyful, unconditional, accepting love, it stirs up the old emotions of loss and rejection. You almost want to pick a fight with them so they will leave you alone. Of course, you don't really want to be left alone (again), but how many people who try to love can stick it out?

Those wounds also keep you from maturing. When you are a chronological and physical adult but still a child or adolescent emotionally, the incongruity baffles most folks. They want you to grow up, but your Type A wounds inhibit that ability.

The inner wounds get overlooked because the outer symptoms are so glaring. But those symptoms aren't the real issue; they're only the evidence of Type A wounds.

My singles pastor was incredibly perceptive. He saw me, really saw me, when others would not. I remember one day, when I was walking across the sanctuary, and he asked how

I was. My response was a noncommittal "Okay." That one word had rescued me many times from being vulnerable. But this day, he literally planted himself in front of me and looked me in the eyes. This was difficult enough in itself because I wouldn't meet his gaze. He persisted, maneuvering side to side and up and down until he managed to gain my focus.

Then it was either elbow him out of my way or stop and feel the grief his loving actions triggered. I didn't want to cause a scene, so I stood still. What was he up to?

"'Okay.' That means 'not good,' doesn't it?"

My surprise overwhelmed my pain. How could he possibly know me that well? It's sad, but too often people who ask "How are you?" don't really want to know. He did.

I don't remember much of what happened after that. Perhaps I dissociated and the little ones took over. Perhaps I was simply so surprised it took a while to regroup.

This was one of the primary wedges driven into my nearly impenetrable wall of pain and defense. The healing journey had not yet begun, but a spiritual adoption was in progress. He became my spiritual father and helped me heal from a Type A wound that the emotionally distant relationship with my earthly father had caused.

John, my counselor, became a spiritual "uncle" to me. I'm sure he knew prayer counseling in and of itself would not be enough for healing, maturing, and growing me into the person God had created me to be. With that in mind, he helped me find other spiritually adoptive "family members" to help move the process along.

You've heard of the book *It Takes a Village*. The title is referring to raising physical children, but it certainly is true for wounded adult children as well.

And who is the chief of our healing village?

Jehovah God. Scripture states, "We love, because He first loved us" (1 John 4:19 NIV).

You can feel it when a person loves you with God's love. Even through anger or disappointment, love is still there. It's there in their eyes, in their voice, and in their touch. And somehow, it leads you back to the *Agape* Source.

Have you ever felt love emanating from a perfect stranger? I believe it's only happened to me once.

Peter Marshall Jr. was guest speaker at my college chapel service during my freshman year. My 8:30 a.m. biology class had ended a few minutes early, and I had gone directly to the sanctuary. I stopped at the entrance to scan the nearly empty room, stepped inside, and saw our speaker on the platform, readying himself for his talk. Two steps closer and he glanced at me.

My heart melted. He was at least fifteen feet away, but I could feel his loving spirit reaching out to me. It felt a bit like a cool breeze on a hot day. I sat and basked. I practically floated out the door afterward.

The proof of love is in both words and actions. Jesus' love can counter the lies we believe, no matter how long they've been there. It can heal the pain.

Jesus was a total stranger to the little ones who were trapped in a painful memory. They wouldn't just jump into His arms when invited. Pain and torment were real to them; love was not. Lies were what they had always heard, not reassurances of His tender *agape*.

John tried to describe Jesus to the little ones, tried to present Him in spirit and in truth. Whether or not they received the words was always up to them.

The little ones believed the true Jesus would hurt them, just as the false ones had. One by one He proved to them He wouldn't.

Angry little one: *What good are You? You never help. You just stand around and watch!*

Oh, I'm afraid He's going to hurt me now.

John: He's not going to hurt you, are You, Lord Jesus? *(pause)* What's He doing?

Little one: *Nothing. I thought He'd hurt me, but He didn't.*

John: What are you feeling? Lord Jesus, would You show her?

Little one: *Feelings don't matter anyway. I can't even see Him. I've got my eyes closed 'cause I thought He would hurt me.*

But He's still not mad at me!

Since they had never been protected against the torment, the little ones didn't believe Jesus would be willing or able to do it.

It's like I'm lying on his hand, and his hand is big enough for all of me. And it's warm and it's soft. And I don't have to be afraid anymore.

John: That's the truth.

And now He's holding me, and I can hear His heart. Such love on His face. And He said, "You're gonna grow up, and I'm gonna be with you all the way. You won't always see me, but I'll always be there, 'cause I love you and you belong to me and not to them!"

The little ones worried that they were living in a fantasy world. That (and dissociation) was their only defense against the reality of ritual abuse.

> Little ones: *We're just making this up; it's not real. None of this is real!*
>
> John: Is that true, Holy Spirit? Are they making up all this pain?
>
> Little one: *If I say it's not real, they won't hurt me anymore. It's coming from all sides and all I can do is go inside. I don't know what else to do.*
>
> John: What happens when you go inside [dissociate]?
>
> Little one: *I don't feel it so much.*
>
> John: But it's still there?
>
> Little one: *Yeah...*

It just stopped. Everything just stopped. There's no sound, but Jesus just walked in. He doesn't lie. He doesn't hurt little girls. He wants to help. He wants to be a Daddy that won't hurt us.

God is love. He loves us. And His love heals, reaching us individually in a way He knows we can receive. I found this to be true for the little ones, as well as for the adult me.

Sometimes His love reaches us in a roundabout way . . .

"See ya!"

"Bye. Glad you came. Drive careful." Several of my friends called out as I left the meeting. Driving home across town, I had to go slightly north and then due west into the setting sun. I hadn't really wanted to come in the first place, but they had expected me.

The overpass curved to the left. No guardrails. I could speed up a little, miss the curve, and sail off into oblivion. It would be so easy. People died in car accidents all the time. No one would think it was suicide.

I shook my head, trying to clear the mental darkness. I had to get home. Had to go back to work tomorrow. People needed me. But no one knew my needs . . .

Repeated suicidal thoughts dated back to childhood. Only two things had kept me from following through during my late teens: my mom's devastating grief at losing her youngest and my worry of ending up in hell.

Adulthood was no better. Prolonged peace had never been in my emotional repertoire.

And now my latest counseling session had shattered my life all over again. My heart was deadened. My tears remained unshed.

I shoved my problems aside. My patients' issues took priority over mine. Daily, I returned home to hide, exhausted.

Nothing helped. Faith was a mirage.

Trickling doubt became a tsunami. Had God forgotten me?

Getting ready for work every morning was like slogging through Jell-O. No one knew suicide shadowed me—not colleagues and certainly not patients.

No one but God.

I usually ate lunch at my desk. That day was no different.

"Hello?" My office phone showed a Texas number.

"Hey, sistah." Carla's smooth southern drawl came through the wires. My old coworker and encourager hadn't called in three years.

"Carla? How did you get this number?"

"Oh, I have my ways. Heard you've been going through a rough time."

I nodded in silence as tears prickled behind my eyelids.

"I had a dream last night. You were wandering around lost inside that church with the stained-glass window. Remember?"

Lost. That was me.

"Jesus is still holding on to you. Don't give up, hon. Please don't give up."

The dam burst. Tears withheld for weeks flowed.

I wasn't abandoned. Jesus knew right where I was.

And He'd assigned Carla to throw me a long-distance lifeline.

Sometimes God's love is forthright and straight from His heart to ours:

Phil Driscoll has been a fantastic trumpeter for God—literally. He plays the trumpet in worship, and was very well-known in the '90s. On this Sunday he was a guest musician at my large church. At one point, he spoke about his son, also a trumpet player. He said he loved to hear his son play because he was a reflection of him. That's how God sees us, he added.

Then he started to play.

I don't recall the song. What I do remember is receiving an incredible baptism of love from the Father lingering well beyond the song.

In my mind's eye, I saw a party favor. When I raised my hands or my voice in worship, it curled back toward me. But when I relaxed and simply opened my heart, it straightened out and became a silver conduit for Father's love to flow through. It gushed like an open fire hydrant and inundated me. I wept through the entire service, barely pulling myself together at the end.

I'd been asking God to let me feel His love for years. This went way beyond any expectations.

Few people remained in the sanctuary as I stood, dumbfounded and silent.

"You've been crying." What could my choir director be thinking? I hardly ever cried.

"Yeah. Anybody who saw me probably thought something really bad happened."

"Oh, no." He shook his head, smiling gently. "I could tell. It was something really good."

So, hard-pressed not to start sobbing again, I told him what had transpired.

That episode was the culmination of decades of yearning for God's love, while still doubting and downright refusing it. I had once told Him I loved Him during worship and felt Him reply, as if from a distance, "I love you too." It scared me so much I pushed it away. Never tried it again.

How could God love me after all I'd been through?

What about all my fear? My pain?

That experience was another preparation for the healing journey I started a few years later. The journey was hard, even painful at times. But most of the time, when I had nothing else to hold on to, I knew God's love was still there.

Gradually, the fear and pain were replaced by trust and confidence. I discovered I wasn't crazy. There were real causes for my pain, for the gaps in my memory, and for the distorted emotions.

Slowly I mended and grew and learned.

I finally accepted God's love.

16

Forgiveness

I survived the most heinous form of abuse ever invented. My abusers stole my childhood, my identity, my very soul.

The damage they left me with kept me from living a normal life. Few friends, minimal social life, negligible emotional stability, sporadic episodes of peace. It seemed all I had left was my intellect and my redeemed spirit.

Once I discovered what had actually happened, I couldn't talk about it for fear of being thought crazy. I kept my own family in the dark.

The more I learned about the rituals and abuse, the more I hated those people. When I learned Nazi Germany's Josef Mengele was one of the role models for their activities, rage fought with hopelessness and depression.

Oh, I didn't die, but I wanted to. Came very near to suicide lots of times. Even made a plan, but then put it on a mental shelf. Thinking about what that kind of loss would do to my mom stopped me. And what would God think about it? I was a Christian but didn't trust Him very much.

But those despicable men had to pay for what they had done to me.

Masonic symbols seemed to be everywhere. I saw belt buckles, rings, bumper stickers, advertisements, hats... you name it.

Every time I saw a square and compass symbol, my stomach tightened. Sometimes I broke out in a cold sweat. Whenever I drove past a Masonic temple, bile rose. Hatred raised its ugly head.

Justified, right?

"Love your enemies, and pray for those who despitefully use you" (Matthew 5:44, paraphrased).

Wait—what? I was supposed to forgive them?

God, are You kidding?

How could I forget what they did? How could I let them off the hook?

It took a while before I realized I just didn't understand forgiveness. Frankly, I didn't know if I wanted to. But, eventually, I learned.

Let's start with these misconceptions:

1. *You have to forgive and forget.*

    This is impossible. We literally can't forget, unless we repress the memories. Even then they remain in storage. Think of the results if we did forget: it would be like the movie *Groundhog Day*. We would have no defense against the situation being repeated. No idea of how to help someone else. And the memories would return to storage, beginning the cycle of torment yet again.

Forgiveness

2. *We need to pretend it never happened or that it wasn't as bad as we thought.*

   This would make us live a lie. Of course it was bad, and we know it. We were badly hurt and we still live with the results. Our souls would outright reject that lie.

3. *You should let the perpetrator off the hook.*

   This would entail making excuses, like "He was abused as a child," or "He has a quick temper," or worst of all, "I deserved it."

Oh, really? There are a lot of people who suffered abuse without becoming abusers. Lots grew up in an atmosphere of violence and anger. They learned to control their tempers instead of letting their tempers control them. And nobody deserves abuse or assault.

All of these false perceptions are destructive and re-traumatizing. They negate our honest emotions and dishonor us as people.

So, now we know what forgiveness isn't. But what is it, exactly? I like how my Okie pastor puts it: forgiveness is giving up your right to get even.

Simply put, forgiving is allowing God, the only true and righteous Judge, to do His job. We were never given the authority to assume that role.

Have you ever judged someone harshly and then discovered something that clarified their actions? Maybe even made you feel sorry for them? Yeah, me too.

And it took a while, but what I've learned about forgiveness is this: it's more for our benefit than for the perpetrator.

Consider this: How much does it hurt the other person for you to judge him?

Not at all.

How much does it hurt you to judge him?

Plenty.

I remember an old saying: not forgiving is like drinking poison and believing the other person will die.

Unforgiveness is soul poison. It eats away at us slowly, inexorably, until nothing but the anger and hurt remain. Sometimes we even forget the original offense but still hang on to the pain.

Physically, unforgiveness can lead to illness beyond an acid stomach and a tension headache. Struggling to keep your rage buried is exhausting and stressful to the body. Some evidence exists of a link between certain types of disease and repressed anger. For example, see the September 18, 2017, *Psychology Today* article "Anger and Cancer: Is There a Relationship?" by Robert Enright Ph.D. or the October 2000 Cancer Nursing article "Anger and Cancer: An Analysis of the Linkages" by Sandra Thomas, et al.

It appears that the body sometimes turns on itself and disease occurs due to the toxins that have been bathing the organs. The human body is unable to function properly for long in such a toxic environment.

Emotionally, unforgiveness can easily lead to depression or anxiety. You look at the world through a dark filter. Long-held anger can erupt as unfocused and misdirected fury. Refusing to forgive may manifest as bitterness, which can ultimately cause separation from your loved ones.

Spiritually, unforgiveness comes between you and God; the anger and guilt keep you from approaching Him. It also hinders our prayers. I think it makes the Lord very sad when He sees us try to forgive through our own efforts and

Forgiveness

fail miserably. When we judge ourselves for that failure, His heart hurts for us.

But we simply don't have the power within us to forgive anything beyond basic, mild offenses. To go bigger, we have to make the choice to forgive and we have to use God's strength to do it. This is true whether we are in physical proximity to the person or it all occurs in the spiritual and emotional realms.

I remember walking into John's office one day with a massive chip on my shoulder. Shooting a fierce glare at him, I positioned my water bottle and then myself.

"I really do not want to be here."

"Oh? And why is that?"

"I am just furious at you!" I felt my jaw clench.

He nodded. "Why are you so angry?"

Then I let him have it, both barrels. Although I forced myself to speak in measured tones, my words were straight, sharp, and to the point. He had said something that annoyed me thoroughly at our previous visit. I took it home, mulled it over, and let it grow into anger and then fury over the next two weeks. I judged him without mercy.

Silent now, I resumed glaring at him.

"I'm sorry. I shouldn't have said that. Will you please forgive me?"

Wait—what? His reply shocked me out of my fury. An apology was kind of like hearing a foreign language.

I sighed and then nodded.

He didn't accept that. "I need to hear you say you forgive me."

Not, "You need to forgive me," but, "I need to hear it."

"Okay. I forgive you."

Of course, my confused heart wasn't really in it, but John thanked me and we went on. Only later did I realize that I needed to hear it more than he did.

Whom might you need to forgive? Here are a few suggestions to get you started:

A friend . . . a sibling . . . a parent . . . a spouse or an ex.

Now go deeper:

A minister . . . perpetrators from the recent past . . . or from many years ago.

Deepest:

Yourself . . . Jesus . . . God.

You've probably surmised that most of these are from my own personal experience. Boy, have I had to do a ton of forgiving! A lot of the session notes include my choosing, usually reluctantly, to forgive.

But forgiveness is both a choice and a directive. Paul encouraged the Ephesians and the Colossians to forgive the grievous acts of the brethren (Ephesians 4:32, Colossians 3:13). Jesus told Peter that he was expected to forgive his brother "seventy times seven" rather than the "seven" times noted in the Torah (see Matthew 18:21–22 KJV). It's all our choice whether or not to obey.

So, how do we forgive?

Let's start with something easy. If someone cuts you off in traffic, then gives you a one-finger salute, what do you do? Most of us avoid road rage and just brush it off. But how about praying first? Maybe something like this:

"Lord, that driver acted like a jerk, but I choose to forgive them. I release them to your judgment. And I bless myself with peace." See? You express forgiveness and give yourself the bonus of peace too.

Forgiving gets tougher when it's someone you have trusted. If a good friend chose to betray your trust, her actions hurt you. The wound is deeper and it's harder to forgive. You will have to acknowledge the depth of your pain before you release the person. You might even want to write out what she did and how you feel about it. By the way, read these things aloud before you write "Paid in Full" on the paper and then tear it up. Words have power.

Have you ever seen how easy it is for a little child to forgive? Most release the anger quickly and then go back to playing with the one who hurt them. No grudges. This is as it should be. But a ritually abused child has had too much pain and torment to forgive easily.

While studying the session notes for this chapter, my heart ached for the little girl who had felt so much despair, rage, even hatred . . . and not all of it was directed at the perpetrators. Time after time, John guided me/her toward Jesus, only to have her refuse to engage with Him. Continual encouragement and reassurance eventually combined to convince her to let Jesus into the scene.

> LITTLE ONE: *But if He saw them, why couldn't He stop it? Why didn't anybody help me?!*

> JOHN: Lord Jesus, is it all right if she gets mad at you?

> LITTLE ONE: *I can't, 'cause then He won't do anything.*

JOHN: Is that true, Lord Jesus?

She hesitantly goes over to Him, fearing her own rage.

LITTLE ONE: *Why did You let this happen! You could've protected me! You didn't have to let any of it happen. You could have stopped it; You could have made those* wolves [evil spirits influencing the church people] *go away. You let them hurt little kids and then You try to make up for it!*

It's bad enough what they do outside, but You let them do it inside . . . It's supposed to be Your house and You're supposed to be in control. You don't care. You let them go anywhere they want to. You didn't make a safe place for us, so we have to take care of ourselves 'cause You don't care!

Wait. He's crying. Did I hurt Him that much?

JOHN: Lord Jesus, why are you crying?

LITTLE ONE: *It's 'cause He loves me, and I hurt so He hurts. . . . But He didn't stop it! If He loved me that much, why didn't He stop it?!*

He says He couldn't stop it, but I don't understand why. And I don't want to hear "He couldn't do it," because He's powerful and He's strong and He should be able to do it! I just want to put my hands over my ears and yell "No, no, no!"

JOHN: You can choose to do that, but I think He has something more to say to you.

LITTLE ONE: *I'm too mad at Him!*

JOHN: Yes, but would you be willing to forgive Him?

LITTLE ONE: *That doesn't seem right, 'cause He's big. He forgives people. He doesn't need me to forgive Him.*

JOHN: Jesus, is that the truth?

She shakes her head.

LITTLE ONE: *Maybe I can . . . . How can I do that?*

JOHN: Just tell Him you're willing to forgive Him.

She did. And then she listened. And she heard:

LITTLE ONE: *He made me a little kid, so I was supposed to be here. But they took it away. And we tried so hard to be big enough, but we couldn't do it. We failed to protect her.*

NARRATOR: *And Jesus told her, "It's not wrong to fail. None of this was your fault."*

Then came the day when I challenged John, spitting out the words after a mid-session break.

"God let those monsters do whatever they wanted! Doesn't seem like He cares much, huh?"

Contempt for the Creator mingled with fear of His wrath.

The ever-patient John waited for my emotional frenzy to subside. He drank some water and watched me for signs of dissociation.

My gaze shifted upward, waiting for a lightning bolt to come crashing through the ceiling and devour me for blasphemy.

Never happened.

John closed his laptop and stood. "How about we go for coffee?"

Wordlessly, I nodded and rose. Just what was he planning? Was he going to talk about my forgiving God? We'd gone through that plenty of times. But this was anger from the adult me, not in the memory of the child.

We headed for Starbucks, walking across the street and around the grocery store. An empty table waited in the shade outside. We got our drinks and then sat in silence for a bit.

"Huge anger." He spoke in a gentle tone.

I nodded.

"Anger at God?"

Another outburst. "Do you blame me? I could have done a better job with my life than that!"

"Maybe. Maybe not. But it wasn't your job to do." John sipped his latte.

A growl escaped my clenched jaw.

"You have a perfect right to be angry, you know. And to tell Jesus about it. Yell, scream, cry, accuse. He can take it all. He knows how you feel, anyway, so why not?"

"You think I want to make Him mad at me? No way."

Our remaining time flew by as John encouraged me to be honest with myself and with God. "Psalm 51:6 says He

Forgiveness

desires truth in the inward parts and in the inward parts He will make us know wisdom . . ."

He wrote the reference on a napkin and handed it to me. "Read this when you get home. Study it. Let it sink into your heart before you try to confront the Lord."

"Okay." I reluctantly shoved the napkin into my jeans pocket.

Several days later, homework completed, it was time to contend with God. Time to be honest and ask hard questions. But would it be safe?

I sat cross-legged on my basement floor, rocking back and forth, agitated almost beyond control.

Where was God? And where was He when all this torment and abuse happened?

Could I rage at Him? I seriously wanted to, but I was afraid. Wouldn't that be a big, ugly sin? Maybe even dangerous.

But I followed through, right there on the basement carpet. Raging, crying, even begging for answers, I challenged Him over the next ten minutes. Exhausted, I fell silent.

Still no answers. At least He didn't threaten me with torture and death. Not like the perpetrators.

Why wouldn't God answer my question? What was He waiting for? I thought He loved me!

I raged at God several times over the following weeks. No clear answers.

Exhausted, I finally surrendered my anger to Him. "Oh, God, I'm so tired of all this. You know how I feel. You made my feelings. I don't know what to do now."

I knew why the perpetrators did what they did: a thirst for power, misogyny, addiction to evil, manipulation of spiritual things. It seemed God wouldn't let me know why He hadn't intervened.

I let my mind drift back through the journey. Seeing how certain people had entered my life at just the right time. How teaching material became available when I was ready for it. How many others there were like me; I knew a dozen of them personally.

"God's timing is perfect." Boy, had I gotten tired of hearing that! But now it seemed truer, not just capricious and arbitrary.

I sighed in resignation. "Okay. I don't much like it, but if that's all You have for me . . ."

Wave after wave of anguish washed over me as God let me feel His grief. My Father hated that I had had to wait so long, had to live in such turmoil, until He saw that everything was in order for my healing.

That grief gave me greater understanding in heart and in mind. It helped diminish my rage at God. If He had revealed my past to me when I was in my twenties, there would have been very few healing resources. Most people simply didn't believe ritual abuse was real. Psychology didn't understand the depth of trauma endured by ritual abuse survivors or the magnitude of dissociation resulting from it. Christian counselors and therapists had not yet fully received His revelation of truth on how to work with survivors toward healing.

I wish this was a rare thing. It isn't.

I've been asked a few times if any of my perpetrators received justice.

"Not that I know of. They're probably all dead by now. But we did take them to the court of the righteous Judge, so I know they're not off the hook."

Forgiveness

I have taken many people to "court" and have led others through the process. (For a more complete picture, check the forgiveness PDF on my Cords of Grace website).

Once you feel ready to engage in the "courtroom" process, please don't try to go through it alone; it can be very difficult and emotional. Join with an experienced counselor/minister. Allow plenty of time.

These are the essential concepts:

This is your courtroom. Design it according to your preferences. You are the judge, with bench, robes, gavel, and all. Don't try to say you are not the judge, because you have already put yourself in that position.

The defendant is the person you have judged. He or she is in your courtroom. All the charges against him or her will be listed and presented by the judge. The charges you speak are very real and they are serious. Later, the charges will be forgiven and dismissed.

Jesus is always invited into the courtroom. He makes the decision where to sit or stand. After the charges are dismissed, the defendant is turned over to Jesus.

The judge steps down and goes to Jesus and to the defendant. Forgiveness for judging is requested. The ex-judge offers prayer for the defendant. Ministry occurs.

In the past when I took someone to this court, I inevitably saw Jesus lovingly take my offender outside into the light. When I took the cult to court, I saw Him take them out wearing shackles on wrists and ankles. He was very displeased and would not let them go into the light without dealing with them first.

I understood. I forgave and released them.

The righteous Judge took over.

17

Reintegration

Have you ever felt as though Scripture existed to make you uncomfortable? That it held nothing meaningful for you? Has it been more like a textbook than the living Word of God?

Boy, count me in on that one. As a dissociative, I felt particularly condemned by the concept of being "double-minded." How could someone with dissociation and alternate personalities get past the obvious?

I was literally of two (or more) minds. How could I muster up enough faith to please God? How could I ever expect any prayers to be answered while in that condition?

My emotional torment arose from these passages (all emphasis is mine):

> But if any of you lacks wisdom, let him ask from God, who gives to all freely and with no reproach, and it will be given to him. But let him ask in faith, doubting nothing. For the one who doubts is like a wave of the sea, being driven by wind and being tossed; for do not let that man suppose that he will receive anything from the Lord; *he is a double-souled*

man, not dependable in all his ways. (James 1:5–8, The Literal Translation)

Draw near to God, and He will draw near to you. Cleanse your hands, sinners! *And purify your hearts, double minded ones!* (James 4:8, The Literal Translation)

The King James Version says it this way:

Draw nigh to God, and he will draw nigh to you. *Cleanse your hands, ye sinners; and purify your hearts, ye double minded.*

Was I living in the sin of double-mindedness because my mind was fragmented into multiple parts? What a dilemma!

Of course, I have chosen to be double-minded on occasion, just like the Israelites of the Bible and many modern-day Christians. I've wondered if God really existed—and if he did exist, did He care about me?

Sometimes I've held the attitude of "What has He done for me lately?" I've waffled between anger, rebellion, and plain old doubt. And I've wondered if going my own way would be better than struggling to follow His.

But I've also discovered that being dissociative, no matter how many parts you have, is not the same as being double-minded. It doesn't cause a lack of faith.

Salvation of the spirit by accepting Christ is a "one and done." Our spirits are made pure at that moment, and the decision is made by the core person.

The "salvation" of our souls is quite different. Paul wrote about this in Romans 12:2, telling us not to be conformed to the world but to be transformed by the renewing of our minds (which are contained within our souls: mind, will, emotions). Soul sanctification is a lifelong process.

This is seriously good news! Having parts does not disqualify you from hearing God or receiving answers to prayer. It does not make you double-minded. Our choices do that.

Jeremiah 17:5 states that God declares, "Cursed is the man who trusts in man, and who makes flesh his arm, and who turns aside his heart from Jehovah" (LITV). In other words, believing in ourselves over believing in God's strength curses our endeavors.

This is being double-minded, and God is not punishing us for it but is explaining the natural consequences of this kind of disobedience and lack of faith.

Double-mindedness is a sinful choice. Having parts is not a sinful choice but one of survival.

Just as having parts is not sinful, being reintegrated does not lead to righteousness. So why all the hoopla about achieving reintegration?

Although reintegration is not the ultimate goal of therapy, it is an incredibly good thing. As I've said previously, healing is the ultimate goal, and reintegration is an important part of the healing process. The dissociated parts/alters often guard prophecies, promises, or gifts that have not been utilized until now. Reintegration frees those guardians (along with their gifts) to be an active, working part of us.

Reintegration happens in a myriad of ways. Some are obvious, some more subtle. It can involve one or many little ones.

And it's different almost every time it happens.

Reintegration

Occasionally, one or more little ones convince some of the others that it's time to take action. At that point, it's a group decision.

I have heard of alters walking up a path and then disappearing into Jesus. Sometimes, He hugs them and they melt into Him. Or He leads them to the core person and they step directly into her. They might grow up while Jesus is with them and then come into the core person. And since Jesus lives in me, if they go into Him, they reintegrate—into me!

It doesn't matter a bit exactly how it happens, only that it does.

In going back through my session notes, I discovered several instances of reintegration. Some made me chuckle, some led me to say an "aah" of appreciation.

June 2002

He [Jesus] wasn't mad at the other perpetrators so much, but the false jesus, well, He just blasted him.

"How dare you! How dare you take My name and use it against this little one!"

Then He picked her up off the table and He's holding her again. He says, "Don't be afraid. I am here and I am real and you don't have to be afraid anymore."

I was watching and I looked up into His face. It was so kind. I smiled at Him and asked if we could bring her [the little one] over again and He said, "Sure." It was like pulling a balloon over with a string and He brought us together. There isn't two of us anymore, there's just one.

January 2003

The little one/alter was so exhausted and frightened of the torment that she felt it would be better to be dead. She said as much to Jesus.

Then He told her, "If you're dead you can't feel the pain, but you can't feel anything else, either."

She said, "I don't think I want to feel it, though. I was so scared! I don't want to hurt anymore, but that's all that's there. If it's gone, there'll be nothing left."

John asked Jesus if that was true.

The little one heard Him answer.

He said that's all there's room for now, but if He takes it away there'll be room for other things. I see . . . It's like when you have a water jar and you push the button at the bottom and water runs out. It's 'cause pain is heavy and it has to go out the bottom and the other feelings are lighter and they go in the top. I don't know what they are but He said it was okay.

She laughed.

Then the little one asked, "Can we leave now?"

Jesus said "Yes."

They walked off hand in hand and she was skipping!

June 2003

I can't get back in [into the memory]. I'm stuck, halfway in and halfway out. Someone's pulling on me. The little ones are pulling on me. They don't want me to go in there; they know I'll get hurt.

If anybody ever finds out about this they're gonna hate me. They're gonna reject me.

The bad men said, "We have to divide the good part from the bad part. The bad part can never be seen; nobody can ever see it."

They told me that they're good and they hurt us to make us better.

"If you leave us, it'll never get better."

These are the only people that can see the bad part and still accept me!

I see that big, gray blob again. Jesus picked it up. He's getting real close and He's blowing on it. And it's melting into a person. Into me. I didn't know it but it was part of me the whole time.

September 2003

This memory contained several demonic figures. The little ones have met Jesus, and now they refuse to obey the guardians anymore.

John asked, "Would you like to tell those bad men [demonic guardians] to leave?"

Yes. (And I could just see them standing straight with their little fists clenched and stomping a foot.)

"Holy Spirit, show them how."

We're not scared of you anymore and Jesus says, "Go away!" So, go away!

Jesus said that wherever they were, they're gone, so it's ours! And we can do whatever we want!

> ADULT PERSONA: *One little one is out now, and I can see her running from one side of the open space to the other. She's playing. When Jesus is there, it's safe to play.*

They're fine now, but I feel such a sense of loss. And if He takes that away, what does that leave me?

John asked, "What do You say about that, Jesus?"

"It's legitimate. And it won't be there forever."

But I feel so separate from all the little ones. It's like they're strangers.

Would you like the Lord to bring you together? He can do that.

I nodded and waited. Finally, I said, "That filled some of the emptiness. Some of them are still out there, but some are here together (with me). It's nice."

September 2006

There's a demonic guardian in the caves. The little ones could never see him before, but now he scares them. He's like a jail warden keeping the prisoners in line.

Jesus went into the cave and grabbed the guardian by the throat. Then He shook him and took Him out into the light. The light melted him.

When the little ones saw that happen, about a dozen hurried out of the cave and into the light where Jesus was standing. They were climbing all over him, laughing and playing. He laughed, too, enjoying their antics like any good father would.

This was fun! They don't want to go back into the dark cave. Then He waved His arm and it was like massive erosion as all the caves closed.

They're so very little and now they want their mommy. They all came over and joined with me. They feel safe now; it seems they know I was protecting them all this time.

What did Jesus think of all this? He simply told me I was a good mom.

I have had some remarkable experiences of reintegration. One in particular stands out in my memory:

About twenty little ones came out of their hiding places in a warren of caves in response to Jesus calling them. They all went with him into the sunlight. Then John asked the Holy Spirit if He wanted to do something to prevent the little ones from going back into the caves now that they knew they could trust Jesus.

At that point, I saw the caves collapse into a huge pit. Some dust rose from the event, but not enough to obscure my mind's vision as I saw the pit fill with water. I couldn't see any source, but clearly it symbolized the presence of the Holy Spirit. Things got really interesting once the pit was full.

From my left, I heard a cry: "Last one in's a rotten egg!" The little ones ran into view and rushed to jump into the water, laughing and yelling with joy. And I felt it—physically—in my belly. The jolt didn't hurt, but it sure was strong. And who could resist laughing at the antics of the little ones? I couldn't, and neither could John.

We chuckled and giggled for quite a while, renewing the merriment whenever we thought about what had happened. It was so great! We still get tickled about it on occasion.

More important than the reintegration itself was the healing presence of Jesus. His light and His love restored their lives. They went from being terrified and helpless to happy and strong.

Apparently, the little ones had been hanging out with Him long enough. They were ready to "jump in with both feet."

This was a wonderful but fairly rare occurrence. Most of the time, the little ones join Jesus whether they come out on their own or He goes in to rescue them. They love being with Him once they've decided He's safe. And because they are having such a good time, they don't always want to "come in."

They're just like children who've been raised in an inner-city, gang-infested area who have finally been allowed to play in nature. They are exploring their newfound freedom. They are playing in a safe environment with Someone who loves them.

Would you want to go back to the old, unsafe, dark place where you have to hide? Neither do they. And there's nothing wrong with that.

Believe it or not, the little ones actually decide when it's time to reintegrate. It's not up to the counselor or the core persona.

Am I fully reintegrated yet? I don't know, though I do feel less scattered. My mind is quieter.

I suspect the question will remain until I get to heaven. A few alters might be lingering, because I still get triggered on occasion and wonder who is feeling what.

Jesus knows all about them. Until I hear otherwise, I'll leave it up to Him.

THE DANCE

Once more the music swells, And we dance—He and I . . .
The pas de deux.
He has taught me this dance—
I, who was so clumsy. So awkward. So angry and
    withdrawn.
He reached for me, seeing me through the crowd.
He gently led me out, past Condemning eyes, harsh words,
    hands that hurt;
He comforted the frightened child; dried my tears,
    soothed my fears,
Taught me . . . The Dance.

Slowly at first, one step at a time.
Never judging me for falling, No complaints when I
    stepped on His foot,
No laughter at my clumsiness,
As gradually, so carefully, He encouraged me . . . to Dance.

The music swells, and we dance.
His eyes meet mine; We share a secret glance;
I leap into His arms, He catches and lifts me
Effortlessly—
I have no fear . . . His grip is sure, His arms are strong,
His love never failing.

I spin; He steadies me,
His movements in concert with mine, An inseparable pair.
His eyes fill with pride—I have learned the Dance.

My Personal Holocaust

The music swells, He steps aside.
I dance away into the crowd of novices.
Is that fear I see in their eyes? Longing? Perhaps admiration?
I feel His eyes on me as I dance among them,
As I show them what He taught me . . . the Dance.

As He encouraged me, I encourage them . . . Yes, you can dance, too!
I lead those who will follow; lead them to the Teacher,
Show them how to dance with Him.
I love their delight, I enjoy their eagerness,
But I always return to the One with whom I dance.
To feel His strong yet gentle touch,
To know His deep love;
The love we share at . . .

The Dance.

18

The End

ADULT NARRATOR: *Walking through the caves, I sensed a very strong Presence. I keep getting these assurances of how pleased God is that I've been focused on Him during this whole time.*

I felt a split. Felt some fear. Then I got to a big bowl.

JOHN: What's happening, Holy Spirit?

NARRATOR: *There's a big bowl. And some little ones are in there and they keep sliding back in as they try to get out. They're hollering for help and no one hears them.*

JOHN: What's the feeling?

Despair.

JOHN: Would you like to invite Jesus in there?

ADULT NARRATOR: *This is so weird. It feels like I'm supposed to get them out and take them to Him. I don't know how to do that. They need a ladder.*

And as soon as I said, "they need a ladder," there was a ladder. They started climbing up and there was a little one that needed help climbing the ladder. And then I said, "Okay, Lord, where are You so I can bring them to you?

They were so happy to see me. Then I saw Jesus and He welcomed them to Himself saying, "Come on, come on."

Then they were all out in the sunshine and I was still there in the cave and I asked, "God, how come I'm still in the cave?"

He said, "It's okay. You can come and go!"

And with that, John burst into laughter.
I watched him for a moment, then asked, "Uh, what?"
"It means you don't need me anymore!"

John and I met a few more times to tie up loose ends. I learned more about how to minister to my remaining little ones.

Years went by. I had the occasional appointment with John. He called them "tune-ups," sort of like when your car seems to be running normally, but a little "something" calls for your attention.

John has become a resource and a mentor.

And we are still good friends.

Epilogue

Whew! I can hardly believe I squished so much of my life into eighteen chapters! Let's catch up, shall we?

I mentioned working with counseling clients in chapter 10. I'm not functioning in that role anymore, but that doesn't mean I'll never return to it.

My mom had a stroke in 2018 and I moved her into my home; I became her sole caregiver (with some help from home health aides), caring for her until her death in 2022. She was my best friend, and I still miss her.

Since then, I have resumed caring for my own health and wellness. Eating right, working out, the whole nine yards . . . most of the time. And writing, of course.

I don't have "crying dreams" anymore. The deep, inconsolable grief is gone. I do still battle some shame and fear, but I think that's more of a habit now. It's not really a part of me.

The deep rage is definitely lessened. I'm learning how to discern when anger is an appropriate response. Most people learn how to handle emotions at a young age; survivors repress them in self-defense.

Spiritual attacks are very rare, and nightmares nonexistent. No more flashbacks. No more switching. The dissociation is resolved. It has become very difficult, if not impossible, for me to choose to dissociate; it just isn't a default response anymore. I do continue to have some PTSD symptoms (like hypervigilance), but it's not worrisome. Just annoying.

As I mentioned in chapter 17 ("Reintegration"), my mind is mostly quiet now. I'm still me, only more complete and stable, quirky sense of humor and all.

I've been working with material from Restoration in Christ Ministries to clean up deep, leftover wounds. When I do get triggered and can't deal with it on my own, I call on John for help. When the team (God, John, and me) gets together again, it's amazing how God continues to heal.

It's so much easier to pray and worship now. And that ease applies to accepting God's love. It's awesome to be able to feel His loving presence when I am alone and know without a doubt that it's for me. That it's real and I don't have to earn it. And that it won't change.

My passion is to see others healed and restored from the unspeakable horrors they, like me, have endured. Presenting my story and teaching this material to groups, churches, and book clubs will be a large part of that effort. I will also resume writing the blog on my website, Cords of Grace. When you go there, you will notice my store and the multiple PDFs available. Most contain bite-size pieces of the material from this book.

Once this memoir is published and distributed, I plan to update, revise, and publish my three supernatural suspense novels. And maybe write another!

Oh, and one more thing:

About halfway through my journey, I had a vision of an army of healed survivors putting the enemy's forces to flight. I believe this was a true prophecy. When we are healed, we know our God, we know and utilize our authority without fear, and we are justifiably enraged at the enemy. We won't take his torment anymore. Where we once fought for survival, we will now fight for ultimate victory. Vengeance belongs to the Lord, but I believe we will have a hand in it.

Epilogue

Thanks for taking the time to join me. I pray blessings on your journey.

Continue with the Lord. Be strong.

Victory will be yours.

APPENDIX A

A Summary for Survivors

Why do some receive greater degrees of healing? I'm sure there are multiple explanations why some survivors reach higher levels of healing while others, well, not so much. We could give ourselves serious headaches if we tried to sort out each possible reason! A few such factors could include personality types, family structure, length of time of trauma-based mind control/abusive activity, age of survivor during the time the abuse occurred—the list continues.

I asked a couple of wise and trusted fellows for their opinions. Here are some things they brought up as being important to survival and to healing. If you are thinking about entering the healing journey; if you are contemplating your place on the journey; if you want to maximize your opportunities for more complete healing, ask yourself these questions:

1. **Do I want healing badly enough to surrender any apparent reward I receive from my current condition?**

A Summary for Survivors

What rewards can entice you? Sympathy? Someone taking care of you? An excuse not to get involved with people you'd rather avoid? How about the ability you have to wield power over those around you by using your pain and dysfunction? Do you use the blank spaces of dissociation or partial dissociation to manipulate others into cutting you some slack? Does your shame at being dissociative keep you from seeking help?

These gains can be powerful incentives to stay right where you are. Fear is admittedly a large part of that—fear of an unknown future. I once heard a lady ask, "If I get healed, who will I be? And will I like me? Will my friends still like me?"

What that lady didn't understand is that the healed person is still you, only better. I didn't have to give up my intelligence, my quirky sense of humor, or my love of science and literature when I reached a higher level of healing. Jesus did knock off some harsh, rough edges, but my essence is intact. That essence is how He made me, and He called it "good." It was the perpetrators who called it "bad," and then I did the same thing because I believed their lies.

Another lady worried about "losing" her alters if they integrated. They had been protecting her for so many years that she couldn't imagine being safe without them. The truth is this: alters are parts of you. When they integrate at the appropriate time, their presence enhances who you are, and you still have their abilities in place. It's just that you are all the same person now—whole, complete, functioning properly as one, protected by the Lord. Without all the static and walls!

Yet another lady refused to give up her demonic spirit guides. "But they're my friends. They keep me safe!" One would think having demonic influences would never bring gain, but there it was. Knowing they were there made her feel secure. Deep inside, I think she believed the demonic power was stronger than God's. She would prefer to have the false comfort and lies the demonic guides brought her rather than to work through her pain to receive lasting comfort and truth from Jesus Himself.

2. **Do I want healing badly enough to stretch my obedience to the max?**

Obedience can be extremely hard after all the pain and coercion we've gone through. We need to start with our thoughts. Using our spiritual weapons, "we can demolish every deceptive fantasy that opposes God and break through every arrogant attitude that is raised up in defiance of the true knowledge of God. We capture, like prisoners of war, every thought and insist that it bow in obedience to the Anointed One." (2 Corinthians 10:5 TPT). Through obedience we exalt the Lord rather than ourselves.

Any person who practices the manipulation of trauma-based mind control is, to say the least, exalting himself.

And anyone who says, "God can't heal me! Just look at what happened!" or "I can't face Him! I'm too badly defiled!" is doing the same thing. These statements will come up during sessions, but they will be released to the Lord. When survivors hold on to them in daily life, they are putting their own opinions above what God has said. Exalting ourselves has only one focus: idolatry. Worship of us. And that's definite disobedience to the one true God.

What makes you contemplate disobedience? Is it when you are growing tired of the fight, getting angry at your counselor, or fearing you will never reach healing? Is it

A Summary for Survivors

a deep, unexpressed anger at God? Do you have a fear of losing out on some (forgotten) thing the cult promised you? Have you been fooled into thinking that if you feel better, it's time to give up the pursuit?

Been there, done that!

I discovered this journey isn't "crisis management." You have to be in it for the long haul, through good days and bad, for better and for worse. I cannot tell you how many times I had to figuratively grab myself by the collar and drag myself to John's office. Resisting the urge to turn the car around almost became a physical struggle. Sometimes I wanted to so badly! The easy road looked so much better than the tough one.

But God's command was clear, His calling plain: 2 Corinthians 5:18: "Now all these things are from God, who reconciled us to Himself through Christ *and gave us the ministry of reconciliation*" (NASB, emphasis mine). Not only are we called to help folks reconcile with God and others but to help ourselves reconcile internally. The little ones have been separated from one another long enough. They need to be reconciled, to be brought together. And God can't do this without our cooperation and obedience. And He won't interfere with our free will.

John tells me I have a lot of persistence; I sometimes call it pure stubbornness. Ex-pastor Don says that it's tenacity and courage. But I realize now that I just didn't want anything else more than I wanted to be healed. To be "normal." To have a life without the awful memory gaps, pain and shame, and self-hatred. And, yes, to find out how I had gotten so badly damaged. I put one foot in front of the other and walked the path, no matter how long it took. For me, that meant a total of eleven years of biweekly sessions.

Those years were a long, hard, frustrating slog. I remember asking John if this was ever going to end. Through tears of disappointment, I practically begged for reassurance that I could be healed. One email stated: "Yes, you will be healed. I won't give up if you don't. I just don't have any answers about how long it will take. It's different for everybody. And when we do come out the other side, I hope we can still be good friends."

I kept this reassuring email for a long time. And John and I kept going through painful memories and even more painful false beliefs about myself, God, the church, other people, you name it. It was rarely easy; maybe it would be better to say that some sessions were slightly easier than others. But a lie is a lie . . . is a lie. Getting rid of the lies through the love of God eventually healed me.

3. **Am I willing to seek God with my whole heart? Am I willing to minister to others during my journey? Am I willing to comfort others with the same comfort I have received? (See 2 Corinthians 1:4.)**

During my medical training, we had a saying: *Watch one, do one, teach one.*

Translation: *Observe and learn the principle; perform the lesson and learn the mechanics; teach someone else and cement the lesson into your mind and hands.*

It also applies to the healing journey. I learned more as a small group assistant facilitator for Family Foundations International, by ministering as a prayer team participant, and by leading a Bible study and discussion than I ever could have by simply receiving counseling and ministry. John also had me sit in with some of his other clients (with their permission) so I could observe, pray, and sometimes add to the session as I continued to receive healing.

I said yes to other nudges from God that never came to fruition, like preparing to lead a small group in my home. Although I was afraid of having other survivors in my home, I prepared the meeting room and had friends over to pray and anoint the space.

Obedience is the key, and everyone responds differently. We learn from each other. And we learn from seeking after God with our whole hearts, even if our hearts are not yet whole.

4. **Which brings us to the fourth question: Do I want healing badly enough to choose to believe God loves all of me?**

When I say "all of you" I mean all your little ones, but also all of your aspects. I mean He loves your spirit, your soul, your body—YOU. He wants you to know His love in every part of your life, including your relationships, your job, your church, your finances . . . and your past. Are you willing to accept that love even if you don't understand it? Learning to accept God's love was a struggle, but it helped me trust Him.

I still don't completely understand that love. I honestly don't know anyone who does.

IT'S. JUST. TOO. BIG.

Your belief is a choice. It's a choice you need to make on a daily, hourly, even minute-by-minute basis. God loves you. It's a fact. And there isn't a thing you can do to change that. Your feelings have absolutely nothing to do with it.

You know how Scripture can burrow its way into your heart? How it can support you through the tough times?

The verse that I held on to was John 6:68. Here's my interpretation of that story from John 6:

> Many of Jesus' followers had taken offense at His words and walked away, probably muttering under their breath:
>
> "Who does he think he is, talking to us that way? He's just the son of the carpenter Joseph, whom we all know! Son of God, indeed!"
>
> Jesus sat down hard on a sturdy bench and watched them as they left, stiff-backed and angry. His heart ached and a deep sigh lifted his chest.
>
> He looked around and noticed the ones who had remained. His wistful words came straight from His aching heart. "Will you leave me too?"
>
> Then Peter knelt, laid his hand on his teacher's arm, and asked, "Where else would we go, Rabbi? Only you have the words of eternal life. And you trust us enough to share them with us."
>
> The others murmured their assent. Jesus was Messiah.
>
> He loved them. And they, Him.

Although I may have contemplated leaving Jesus, I couldn't. Only He had the words I needed for healing. This I knew.

A Summary for Survivors

When the journey gets painfully difficult (and it will), when you scream out for relief (and you will), when you wonder if healing is even available for you (and you will), make the choice to believe in Jesus' love. Meditate on it. Ask Him to reveal it to you. Ask Him again.

Rest assured He will only reveal it in ways you can receive. And He won't ever reject you.

When you wonder if your search for healing is worthwhile, reach out for help. Don't let the enemy steal your progress, even if you can't see any at the moment.

Don't hide in your darkness any longer. His light waits for you.

All of you.

APPENDIX B

A Summary for Counselors

(Material adapted from Hawkins and Hawkins, *Dissociative Identity Disorder: Recognizing and Restoring the Severely Abused*)

DEFINITIONS

ritual abuse/RA: Per Ron Hawkins of Restoration in Christ Ministries: "The systematic and deliberate infliction of trauma for the express purpose of causing dissociation, which is exploited for a covert agenda involving the use of some form of mind-control programming to direct the thoughts, emotions, body processes and/or behavior of the dissociated parts while leaving the Host completely unaware of the hidden agenda her other dissociated identities are carrying out; or the use of dissociated individuals for such covert projects. This term encompasses Satanic Ritual Abuse (SRA) as well as similar forms of abuse conducted by groups that may not appear to be overtly Satanic. Because of its all-inclusive sense, it is the preferred term used by this author."

dissociation: per Ron Hawkins: "A temporary or prolonged state in which consciousness, identity, memory, and/or perception of the environment may be altered or separated from their usually integrated state. This phenomenon lies on a continuum ranging from normal daydreaming and 'highway hypnosis' on one end to the pathological formation of alternate-identities (DID) at the other end."

SIGNS TO HELP RECOGNIZE DID/SRA

For most survivors, the signs of dissociation are subtle to the observer.

- a shifting of the eyes
- a change of expression not matching the demeanor of the presenting part
- forgetfulness
- exaggerated startle response

MOST COMMON:

- inappropriate responses indicating social discomfort and inability to respond as others do
- always feeling pain even when the person should be happy
- isolation (emotional and often physical)
- inappropriate fear
- mind going blank in response to stress/pressure
- lost periods of time as an adult
- losing objects and inability to be organized, or possible over-organization as a defense mechanism.
- strong fear of men and of intimacy; occasionally, promiscuity, which is likely due to programming
- The most common sign is a lack of childhood memories and/or having large gaps in one's memory.

Examples of questions which may indicate the presence of DID/SRA include:

- Are your emotions uncontrolled or numb?
- Have you felt as though someone else has been controlling your life for a long period of time?
- Have you experienced memory gaps?
- Do you feel completely different from others?
- Do you seek isolation or avoidance of people? Do you experience repeated distrust?
- Does your mind wander or do you frequently lose your train of thought during a conversation?
- Are there changes in your handwriting, (e.g., left versus right handedness)?
- Do you say "us" in reference to yourself?
- Do you hear voices or have intrusive thoughts?
- Do you easily lose touch with your physical surroundings?
- Do you experience unexplained physical sensations or pain? Do you have unexplained bruises, scars, and so on?
- Do you experience repeated failures despite feeling capable?
- Have you noticed a decrease in ability to function without apparent cause?

What Happens to Reveal the Condition in a Survivor's Life?

The perpetrators of RA purposely cause memories to be buried through forced dissociation. On average, the survivor will be in her late thirties or forties when the memories start to "leak." This is when life gets tough, especially for one who has been functioning on a fairly high level.

- She may experience flashbacks or be unable to function normally (for her).
- She may start having nightmares or intense, unfocused fear.
- She may develop symptoms of paranoia.

Although frightening to the survivor, this change is a good sign. It means God thinks she is strong enough to deal with her pain and work toward healing. Remember, He never brings something up without wanting to heal it. This is like saying, "Gotcha" to the enemy. Just when Satan thinks he's winning, it starts to fall apart.

Be aware

In the counseling setting, you will often note that a survivor has a very hard time hearing from God. Usually, this isn't because she has never met Him; it's because she doesn't trust Him. Intense anger or even hatred of Father God is common. The perpetrators of her abuse have invariably worked to convince her that all her pain is His fault.

Often, abusers will have a false jesus present. This person masquerades as the Lord but participates in the abuse, so the victim develops distrust and fear. If you have a person who manifests a strong fear of Jesus, this may be why.

Another common occurrence is misdiagnosis. The symptoms of RA/DID can be mistaken for

- bipolar disease (emotional changes and lability)
- borderline personality disorder (inappropriate social interactions)
- schizophrenia or schizoaffective disorder (hearing voices or having distorted perceptions)
- depression (certainly part of this problem, but not the entire diagnosis)
- post-traumatic stress disorder (hypervigilance, unfocused anxiety)

If a client comes in with a self-diagnosis of schizophrenia, PTSD, bipolar disorder, or borderline personality disorder, she may actually be a survivor. Please be aware that this may be inaccurate, or it may be a case of factitious disorder. People want answers and will accept a diagnosis of mental illness just to have one.

Summary

1. Dissociation is a protective response to severe trauma. It is not generally a sign of mental illness but of a strong mind.
2. The memories are sequestered in a divided mind. They will not fully come forward until God allows it. *Any therapy that forces repressed memories to be exposed re-traumatizes the survivor.*
3. Reintegration (see chapter 17) is not the only goal of ministry/therapy. As the pain is healed and the person learns the truth, reintegration will happen naturally. It should not be a struggle.
4. Working with a survivor is a long-term commitment. It may take many years for significant healing

A Summary for Counselors

to occur. It may take a year or more for the survivor to simply learn to trust the counselor.
5. Working with a survivor can be frightening, frustrating, and exhausting. Trusting God doesn't come easily to survivors.
6. Ministers/counselors have to constantly ask God what to say, what to ask, how to pray.
7. There may indeed be demonic involvement or attachment (see chapter 12). Demons probably will not go willingly, but Jesus' blood overcomes the enemy. His power is infinitely greater than theirs.
8. If in doubt, ask questions! It's better to talk to someone more experienced in this ministry than to wonder if you are in over your head.

If you see a counselee for a period of time with little to no improvement and then discover she is a survivor, don't beat yourself up. You have not harmed her, except perhaps to reinforce programming. She is a SURVIVOR, in more ways than the obvious. Send her on with an appropriate referral and with reassurances that you will continue to pray for her. Encourage and remind her that she has not failed. Neither have you.

The same principles apply to a client who is male.

APPENDIX C

A Summary for Church Leaders

Since there is no truly effective healing treatment through psychology for ritual abuse survivors with dissociative identity disorder, the church is the only hospital available. I am not against secular psychology or Christian psychiatrists, but they are limited in their treatment modalities and results. Helping a client learn to cope with intrusive thoughts, self-condemnation, and nightmares does not equal true healing.

I believe true spiritual contact with a loving God is the only way to healing. The Creator can re-create what has been damaged and restore what has been stolen. He can rewire the brain according to His original blueprint. Neuroplasticity is a thing!

But consider this: "Religion" not only does not heal; it can hurt. Rather than taking part in healing, the church historically has added to the pain of the survivor.

Just going to church can be an ordeal. Deep inside, we know the answers are there somewhere (so we really need to be in church), but fighting through the fear and fatigue and confusion and suspicion can be overwhelming. We fear being in the presence of God and His people, and we don't understand why. We feel confused. Sudden fatigue will attack our bodies and minds. We can't trust anyone,

A Summary for Church Leaders

human or God. Various parts of the services cause unexplained fear, even panic.

These feelings come from within; they are programmed into us by the cult. They come from demonic influences, or they are repressed memories of pain and fear.

Once we are within the church, the teachings themselves can cause more pain:

We are taught to trust God with our troubles. But how can we, when (to us) He has been proven untrustworthy? I have gone through buried memories of being tormented and then being told to call on God for help. Then the tormentors resumed the pain, often electric shock, as punishment for my calling on God. They say, "See what happens when you call for help from God? He doesn't come. He doesn't care about you!"

The lie they teach: God is a tyrant and a bully, an uncaring distant entity.

Another memory for me was of being forced to choose which of the "gods" presented to me was the real god. There were pictures and idols representing Baal, Buddha, Shiva, Baphomet, and others, even Jesus. The perpetrators forced me to kneel in a wire square in front of the idols. Whenever I moved enough to touch the edge of the square, I received an electric shock. Every choice of a god brought punishment; there were no true gods and no correct choices offered. The cult was its own god.

To call on Jesus is no easier. The cult uses the image of Jesus to establish trust and then betray the trusting child. I have gone through multiple memories of someone calling himself Jesus standing next to me through the torment, whispering in my ear, telling me it was good to "leave" (dissociate) from the pain. He told me to only listen to his voice, that he would protect me. At other times he would participate in the torment. Or he would stand a few feet away and ignore me. And he would laugh when I cried. I learned early not to trust in Jesus or anyone else.

The lie: Jesus is not only untrustworthy; He hurts and lies to us.

We are taught to find our answers in the Bible. But reading the Bible has been like reading a textbook for me. It never spoke to me until recently. Hearing other people talk about their devotional time made me feel like something was seriously wrong with me. Several memories have come up where scripture was used to emphasize a point during a "session." The perpetrator would quote scripture, but twist it to justify his actions or to establish his power over me.

The lie: the Bible is only another book.

We are taught that God loves us, that He is our Father, and He wants us to love and worship Him. But what kind of father allows his children to be tortured? What kind of love turns its back on the suffering of the innocents?

The lie: God is powerless to intervene; He doesn't love us, He only pretends to, to trick us.

I still wrestle occasionally with this.

When the true Lord Jesus Christ comes into the memory and brings truth, the little one understands and forgives and comes to him. But in daily life, the adult's anger still rages. Only in increments can we come to forgive Jesus; we believe He allowed these abuses to happen for no good reason, and everything in us screams out for justice. His justice will eventually come to those who perpetrate these things, and I know His anger at them is even stronger than mine.

But God knows my heart; he accepts my rage and does not condemn me for it. His love heals the deepest wounds. (Nahum 1:2, 7 ASV: "Jehovah is a jealous God and avengeth;

Jehovah avengeth and is full of wrath; Jehovah takes vengeance on His adversaries, and He reserveth wrath for his enemies . . . Jehovah is good, a stronghold in the day of trouble; and He knoweth them that take refuge in Him.")

We are taught to participate in the sacraments of the church, to remember what Jesus did for us. But the cult made us participate in infant sacrifice and taking the blood in false communion. They made us believe we were as bad as them. How could the blood of Jesus wash that away?

After those memories arose, Communion was very difficult for me to accept for a while; I couldn't get past the visual images and the sounds of the ceremony.

False communion was not the only sacrament they perverted. They also made me take part in ritualistic marriage and insemination, and ritual death and resurrection. They offered me to Lucifer as a living sacrifice and bride.

The cult has learned to pervert all aspects of righteousness into evil, so the sacraments of the church can cause pain, fear, and confusion to the survivor.

We are taught to expect to feel the presence of God and to seek His face. But we are afraid of God, and don't want Him near us. The false gods the cult has used against us have poisoned our hearts against the one true God.

We are taught to listen to God and that if we hear another voice not our own, it is demonic. But survivors hear voices all the time. The alters argue with us and one another. They tell us different things according to their point of view. When we have a time of silence in a church service, I rarely hear true silence. But I usually don't hear demons either.

We are taught to walk by faith, not by our feelings. But we don't have feelings; they have been buried too deeply. And we don't have faith because there is too much fear. So we go by our intellect and do what we think is right. We try to guess what God may want us to do, or be, and until we are able to accept His love, there is no hope of change.

It is exhausting to go through a church service because of the internal conflict. It is a struggle to be a Christian and to try to live up to the expectations of the leadership, God, and ourselves. It's hard to be part of a group when you constantly have to hide the truth.

Inordinate confusion persists in the survivor. She has to learn who she really is. She needs to know and accept her God-given identity, not the false ones she has believed.

I thought I knew who I was and had a strong faith and trust in God. Then the memories started coming back, and I was shaken to my very core. I have had to relearn in my heart what had been learned in my head. I think the faith I have now is actually stronger because I've been tried by fire. And though it's been tempting, I've refused to give up.

I want to encourage church leaders with one simple truth. As you follow God's call on your life, remember that He sees and treats each of His children as individuals. Continually ask Him to help you see them through His eyes.

Please, don't let these wounded ones just give up. See them.

See . . . us.

Bibliography

Campbell, Ron G. *Free from Freemasonry: Understanding "The Craft" and How It Affects Those You Love.* Grand Rapids: Baker, 1999.

Dimsdale, Joel E. *Dark Persuasion: A History of Brainwashing from Pavlov to Social Media.* New Haven, CT: Yale University Press, 2021.

Friesen, James G., E. James Wilder, Anne M. Bierling, Rick Koepcke, and Maribeth Poole. *Living from the Heart Jesus Gave You: A Life Model Book.* East Peoria, IL: Shepherd's House, 2016.

Hawkins, Tom R., and Diane W. Hawkins. *Dissociative Identity Disorder: Recognizing and Restoring the Severely Abused.* Vol. 1, *Psychological Dynamics.* Grottoes, VA: Restoration in Christ Ministries, 2009.

King, Joe, and Sara King. *Freedom from the Effects of Masonry Workbook: A Practical Manual.* Leeds, England.

Leaf, Dr. Caroline. *Switch on Your Brain: The Key to Peak Happiness, Thinking, and Health.* Grand Rapids: Baker Books, 2013.

Silvoso, Ed. *Women, God's Secret Weapon: God's Inspiring Message to Women of Power, Purpose, and Destiny.* Ventura, CA: Regal, 2001.

Shors, Tracey, PhD. *Everyday Trauma: Remapping the Brain's Response to Stress, Anxiety, and Painful Memories for a Better Life.* New York: Flatiron Books, 2021.

Thompson, Curt, MD. *Anatomy of the Soul: Surprising Connections Between Neuroscience and Spiritual Practices That Can Transform Your Life and Relationships.* Carol Stream, IL: Tyndale House, 2010.

About the Author

Carolyn Sherrow considers herself a Colorado native, having moved there as a toddler. She has long been a storyteller in the realm of short stories, articles, skits, and poetry.

Her life has been science-oriented; she earned her bachelors degree in biology at Evangel College (Springfield, MO), and a certificate in secondary education through Metropolitan State College (Denver). Her PA training was through Baylor College of Medicine in Houston. She has also studied counseling, psychology and sociology.

She is trained in Transformation Prayer (Theophostic) ministry, Face to Face ministry (Cross and Sword), and Family Foundations International small group facilitation.

Multiple short-term mission trips to Native American reservations, as well as medical missions with Mercy Ships in the Dominican Republic and with Deborah Ministries in Kenya round out her volunteer service.

She also writes encouraging self-help and ministry material. These appear on her website, Cords of Grace, and the accompanying blog. Informational PDFs are available there, as well.

Ms. Sherrow enjoys trivia and is fond of saying, "I have a great memory for things with absolutely no importance."

Carolyn Sherrow is available to speak to churches and groups, including book clubs. You may contact her through her website for more information.

Notes

Chapter 2

[1] See CF Sherrow, *Basics of Dissociation* (Cords of Grace, 2014). PDF available on the Cords of Grace website: https://cordsofgrace.com/viewproduct/1.

Chapter 3

[2] See Tom R. Hawkins with Diane W. Hawkins, *Dissociative Identity Disorder: Recognizing and Restoring the Severely Abused*, vol. 1, *Psychological Dynamics* (Grottoes, VA: Restoration in Christ Ministries, 2009),180, 185.

[3] Ron G. Campbell, *Free from Freemasonry: Understanding "the Craft" and How It Affects Those You Love* (Grand Rapids: Baker, 1999).

Chapter 4

[4] See Ed Silvoso, *Women: God's Secret Weapon: God's Inspiring Message to Women of Power, Purpose and Destiny* (Ventura, CA: Regal, 2001), 16, 40.

[5] Joe King and Sara King, *Freedom from the Effects of Freemasonry Workbook: A Practical Manual* (UK, n.d.), 39, 44.

Chapter 5

[6] The man in the green robe was some kind of leader; I saw him often during memory work. He was the one who chose me for the ceremonies.

Chapter 8

[7] Hawkins and Hawkins, *Dissociative Identity Disorder*, 177. Used by permission.

[8] See Tracey Shors, PhD, *Everyday Trauma: Remapping the Brain's Response to Stress, Anxiety, and Painful Memories for a Better Life* (New York: Flatiron Books, 2021), 97–98.

[9] The following account is taken from Ellen Barry, "Study Suggests Trauma Stays in Present Tense," Life and Culture, *Denver Post*, December 9, 2023, 8.

Notes

Chapter 9

[10] Soul ties are emotional ties between people on the soul level. They can be holy or unholy and are associated with trauma, sex, love, affection, trust, and so on. For an example, see 1 Samuel 18:1–4. See also CF Sherrow, "Freedom from Toxic Relationships" (PDF), available at the Cords of Grace website: https://cordsofgrace.com/viewproduct/2.

Chapter 12

[11] Hawkins and Hawkins, *Dissociative Identity Disorder*, 182.

Chapter 15

[12] James G. Friesen et al., *Living from the Heart Jesus Gave You: A Life Model Book* (East Peoria, IL: Shepherd's House, 2016), 83–95.